ENCOUNTER AT SEA

ENCOUNTER AT SEA

AND A HEROIC LIFEBOAT JOURNEY

Ichiro Matsunaga

Gordon J. Van Wylen

Kan Sugahara

Sabre Press
an imprint of
Momentum Books, Ltd.

940.545973
MAT

Printed in the United States of America
96   95   94   3   2   1

Sabre Press
an imprint of
Momentum Books, Ltd.
6964 Crooks Road
Troy, Michigan 48098

ISBN: 1-879094-27-4

Library of Congress Cataloging-in-Publication Data

Matsunaga, Ichiro, 1919-
    Encounter at Sea and a heroic lifeboat journey / by Ichiro
Matsunaga, Gordon Van Wylen, Kan Sugahara.
        p.   cm.
    ISBN 1-879094-27-4: $15.95
    1. Van Wylen, Gordon John.   2. Sugahara, Kan, 1929-   . 3.
World War, 1939-1945--Naval operations, American.   4. World War,
1939-1945--Naval operations--Submarine.   5. World War, 1939-
1945--Naval operations, Japanese.   6. Hardhead (Submarine)   7.
Natori (Ship)   8. Survival after airplane accidents, shipwrecks, etc.
9. World War, 1939-1945--Personal narratives, American.   10.
World War, 1939-1945--Personal narratives, Japanese.   I. Van
Wylen, Gordon John.   II. Sugahara, Kan, 1929-   .   III. Title.
D783.5.H33M38   1994
940.54'5973--dc20
                                                    94-5792

The road must be trod, but it will be very hard. And neither strength nor wisdom will carry us far upon it. The quest may be attempted by the weak with as much hope as the strong. Yet such is oft the course of deeds that move the wheels of the world: small hands do them because they must, while the eyes of the great are elsewhere.

–J. R. R. Tolkien
The Fellowship of the Ring

Contents

Preface

When I left the U.S. Navy in March 1946, I put this facet of my life behind me. It wasn't that this had been a bad or disturbing experience. On the contrary, it had been exciting, challenging, and a great learning experience, particularly the two years I had spent aboard the submarine USS *Hardhead*. Instead, I put these events behind me to focus on other goals: graduate school, career, marriage, family, church, and other activities. The experiences of World War II, exciting as they were, faded from my memory.

How unexpected, therefore, forty–eight years later, for me to join Mr. Ichiro Matsunaga in writing this book, for it is the story of an encounter between the *Hardhead* and the Japanese light cruiser, the HIJMS *Natori*. The focal point of the book is the heroic courage and remarkable accomplishments of 195 survivors of the *Natori* as they rowed three hundred miles in twelve days to reach the Philippines. But it is also a story of the realities of war, and how two naval officers, one Japanese and one American, view these events from the perspective of almost five decades.

Mr. Matsunaga, second in command of the lifeboat unit, published a book about these experiences in 1984. Entitled *The Senior Officer*, it was a tribute to Lt. Eiichi Kobayashi, the senior officer present in the lifeboat unit, in recognition of his superb leadership during this voyage. The book became a best-seller in Japan, and to date has had twenty printings.

I learned about this book in 1989 when I attended a reunion, the first ever held, of those who served on the *Hardhead* during World War II. This story both excited and intrigued me. I was excited to learn that there were far more survivors of this encounter than I had realized, and this was a source of great satisfaction. I was intrigued to learn more about the author, and about the experiences of these survivors during this remarkable journey. I therefore wrote Mr. Matsunaga, introducing myself and expressing my desire to know him and learn more about the events he had written about. In a delightful letter I received in response, he told me about himself, how he came to write this book, and that he had visited the United States and met the captain of our submarine, Capt. Fitzhugh McMaster USN (Ret).

In subsequent correspondence, Mr. Matsunaga related that a friend of his, Mr. Kan Sugahara, his junior in the Japanese Naval Academy, had translated the book into English, and that they would send me a copy. Reading this book was a fascinating experience, for it is a story of heroic accomplishments by crew members of the *Natori* and superb leadership by the senior officer in this lifeboat unit. It was also an emotional experience to relive these events and to understand them from the perspective of those we considered the enemy, who experienced much suffering and hardship because of this encounter.

In further correspondence with Mr. Matsunaga I learned that he was eager to have an English language version of this book published in the United States, and he asked if I could help accomplish this. As I considered this, it occurred to me that perhaps Mr. Matsunaga and I, who were antagonists when the encounter took place, could now, as friends, write a book that described the encounter from both points of view. I proposed this to Mr. Matsunaga, and he readily endorsed the idea. We decided that Mr. Matsunaga and I should undertake this as coauthors, with Mr. Sugahara as translator and liaison. I wrote a first draft, which we edited together utilizing the mail and faxed copies. We now present this book to the English-reading public.

Writing this book with Mr. Matsunaga and Mr. Sugahara has been a rewarding experience. It was also a sobering experience to reflect on the encounter and the background, suffering, and tragedies associated with World War II. I have included some of these thoughts in the final section, entitled "Reflections."

While writing, I was struck with the different backgrounds Mr. Matsunaga and I brought to our naval experiences. Mr. Matsunaga was a graduate of the Japanese Naval Academy and had five years of sea duty, with considerable front line experience before this encounter; I was a reserve naval officer, just a year younger, and was on my first war patrol. His father was a graduate of the

Japanese Naval Academy and an admiral in the Japanese Navy; my family had no naval experience, and I was the first generation to attend college.

That we could become good friends, despite these differences and our encounter at sea, suggests that the personal dimensions of war can be quite different from the military and political realities. This friendship with Mr. Matsunaga and Mr. Sugahara was a wonderful serendipity of this joint endeavor.

How quickly time passes, for though the events of the war between Japan and the United States are very real to us, most of the people in Japan and the United States do not have a personal memory of the events. We hope that this book will provide insights into this major conflict, which has shaped many world events and developments since that time, and enable people to better understand the world we live in today.

While writing this book, I was struck by the human dimensions of war, and how people from different cultures are similar in their deepest longings. War does not simply involve people known by their name, rank, and serial number. It involves people with emotions, feelings, aspirations, and loved ones they care deeply about. I hope that the human dimensions presented in this book will inspire and encourage us to think carefully and deliberately about how we can work together to achieve a significant peace in the world.

Mr. Matsunaga, Mr. Sugahara, and I undertook to write this book under unusual circumstances. We have never met; we utilized the mail and fax machines in writing this book. Because Mr. Matsunaga has limited fluency in English, and I have no abilities in Japanese, Mr. Sugahara served as our translator. He filled this role with competence, sensitivity, and grace. As we worked together we learned to understand one another, with our various perspectives and sensitivities, and through this experience became friends, even though we have not met. To Mr. Matsunaga and Mr. Sugahara I express my sincere thanks for their roles in making this a very rewarding and enjoyable experience.

I am deeply grateful to Phyllis Vandervelde, who typed several drafts of the manuscript with professional competence, and also offered timely counsel and gracious encouragement. Beverly Snyder did excellent work in editing an early draft of the manuscript. Tom and Joan Seller did the final editing and design. Their contributions were invaluable, and I am deeply grateful to them. It was a privilege to work with Kyle Scott of Momentum Books, who very ably guided all phases of production. My sincere thanks also to my wife, Margaret, whose counsel, encouragement, and companionship have meant so much to me over the past forty-two years, and were graciously given me as I wrote this book.

December 1993   −Gordon J. Van Wylen

Preface to
The Senior Officer

In August 1944, the HIJMS *Natori*, transporting urgent supplies from the Philippines to Palau (Caroline Islands), was torpedoed by an enemy submarine and sank three hundred nautical miles (about six hundred kilometers) to the east of Samar Island. A friendly medium-attack bomber flew over and dropped a message cylinder. From this we learned that two destroyers were on their way to rescue the survivors.

The navigator, Lt. Eiichi Kobayashi, twenty-seven years old, was the senior officer present. Instinctively and properly, he organized the *Natori* unit of three boats and 195 survivors as a military unit. However, there was neither food (except for some biscuits) nor fresh water. There was no navigation equipment, such as a magnetic compass or sextant, at all. The senior officer then assumed that chances of the boat unit being spotted by the rescue parties were slim, and he declared we would proceed to the Philippines on our own by rowing the boats for fifteen days. Everyone else suggested remaining in the area to await the arrival of the rescue ships, but Lieutenant Kobayashi remained adamant.

Thus, early on the morning of the thirteenth day, the boat unit at last reached Surigao, on the northeastern tip of Mindanao Island. As we had rowed for ten hours a day, without sufficient food and rest, our physical condition was critical when we came ashore. I believe the successful return of the boat unit depended entirely on the timely decision made by the senior officer and on the crew's devotion to the voyage at the risk of their lives. Although they opposed the senior officer's determination at first, they were later convinced.

Throughout the voyage, as the second in command, I was

beside the senior officer at all times. I closely observed how he persuaded the crew to proceed to the Philippines, how he tackled a storm, and how he managed to prevent a mutiny. I honestly thought his command and leadership were exercised ideally. Once his plan was made, he carried it out without becoming sentimental, and observed moderation in dealing with the crew.

After the war, however, when the *Natori* crew gathered for a reunion, I was all the more astonished to learn that some crew members had secretly plotted to assassinate the senior officer. We were packed in small boats like sardines in a can, without food and water or any apparent hope for the future. Under the circumstances, that some people recklessly planned to murder the senior officer, who gave orders to the crew, well illustrates how precarious the conditions were at that time.

In the postwar years, I studied many disasters at sea. My studies revealed that in war or peace, an abundance of people (some research indicates 200,000 people every year) had encountered maritime disasters, and a great number of victims had perished. Many deaths have been attributed to shipwrecks; however, it should be noted that in many cases shipwreck victims have taken their own lives rather than face a monumental struggle for survival. From my experience, I have learned that even in deteriorated physical condition caused by lack of nutrition, a person can continue to live much longer than commonly is thought possible. On the other hand, that same person can be highly susceptible to mental shock, loss of confidence, and disappointment.

According to the navy, it was then considered impossible for the *Natori* crew to row three hundred miles and reach shore without provisions and navigation equipment. Yet, the firm determination of the senior officer and the utmost efforts exerted by the crew made the "impossible" possible. Without giving up and by striving against adversity, cutting through fate, we experienced the adage, "God helps those who help themselves." I would be pleased if this book is of help to those who make group movements, in war or peace, especially when faced with danger.

I would be deeply grateful for any reader's comments about the arbitrary decisions and biases that may be found in this story, and of their experiences of maritime disaster.

1984   –Ichiro Matsunaga

Translator's Note

In summer 1986 I read Ichiro Matsunaga's *The Senior Officer* (Kojinsha Co., Ltd., 1984). I was then secretary to the Safety Promotion Committee of a commercial air carrier in Tokyo; the worldwide aviation industry focused on human factors in aircraft accidents. Airlines were beginning to spend more and more money on the study of command/leadership and cockpit resource management as additional tools to help understand and limit some of these problems.

While I was looking for a leadership example for demonstration (ironically, bad examples were not difficult to find, because they often ended with an incident, or, worse, an accident) I saw an advertisement for *The Senior Officer* in the *Asahi Shinbun* (one of the three major dailies in Japan). I immediately bought a copy and devoured the material in one day, much as a hungry child consumes sweets. I was so impressed with the narrative and touched by the leadership it showed that I decided to get in touch with Mr. Matsunaga to learn more about his inspiring twelve-day rowing hegira.

Some weeks later, I read the book again, taking more time to thoroughly digest the heroic tale. I came to realize that the story was not merely an example of good command/leadership but also an amazing account of the courageous and persistent efforts of the survivors: human triumph over adversity. I felt that we, the Japanese, should be proud of this remarkable accomplishment and became determined to make the story available to English–speaking people.

To realize this aim, I had to first get acquainted with Mr. Matsunaga. I called him, introducing myself as his junior at the

Naval Academy, and requested his permission to mention his book in the company's safety magazine as a superb example of command/leadership. He readily granted my request.

Since then, Matsunaga–san has frequently met with me at the Tokyo International Airport (Haneda) when he comes to downtown Tokyo on business. As we saw more of each other, I discovered that he shared my desire to have his book published in English. As I was to retire soon and acquire some spare time, I agreed to take up the task of translating the book into English.

As I worked on it, I recalled those difficult days as a midshipman third class at the Naval Academy, rowing with a heavy wooden oar almost 5 meters long and 75 millimeters in diameter–the repetitive toil that no graduate from the Naval Academy in the Imperial Japanese Navy can forget! When the translation was about half completed, I felt as if I were among the crew members of the HIJMS *Natori*, rowing the boat with all my might in the vast Pacific Ocean, not sighting land for days.

Translating *The Senior Officer* was both challenging and rewarding. One thorny issue I faced as translator, and later as the conduit between Mr. Matsunaga and Dr. Van Wylen, involved the use of the word *God*. In the original text, Matsunaga–san, a Buddhist, used the term *kami-sama*, which to him means deity. In this tradition, for example, if a warrior dies a heroic death during war and is enshrined in the Yasukuni Shrine in Tokyo, he is considered a god. This has a connotation different from Dr. Van Wylen's Christian understanding of God. We decided to use the singular attribution *God* throughout the English version and respectfully ask the reader to encompass the differing viewpoints of the two principal authors.

During his efforts to acquire an English audience for the book, Mr. Matsunaga met with Capt. Fitzhugh McMaster, USN (Ret). Captain McMaster was the commanding officer of the USS *Hardhead* when it sank the light cruiser *Natori*. I had the honor and opportunity to help bring these distinguished naval officers together, face to face, in Washington, D.C., in November 1988. "Time heals all wounds," and after we had spent a few days together, I realized how much Captain McMaster and Mr. Matsunaga respected and appreciated each other. There were no lingering animosities, even though they had once been engaged in mortal combat.

Later, Captain McMaster introduced us to Dr. Gordon J. Van Wylen, who had also served aboard the USS *Hardhead* and participated in the naval engagement that sank the HIJMS *Natori*. As he states in his preface, Dr. Van Wylen came to collaborate with us in publishing *Encounter at Sea*, based on *The Senior Officer*. Mr. Matsunaga and I are very grateful to Dr. Van Wylen for his enthusiastic and energetic endeavors in this project, and for all he did to enable us to reach our goal of publishing this book.

The fiftieth anniversary of the engagement between the USS *Hardhead* and the HIJMS *Natori* will be in August, 1994. Although I have no religious affiliation, I envisage the souls of Captain Kubota, Lieutenant Kobayashi, and many others who sacrificed their lives in encounters at sea congratulating themselves on the publication of this book jointly written by former adversaries.

I would like to express my sincere gratitude to my friends Captain Art Sparks and his wife, Jennifer Brennan–Sparks. Their kind advice and encouragement were much appreciated, particularly during the final translation and attempts to get this book published.

January 1994   Kan Sugahara

PART ONE

AN INTRODUCTION TO TWO SHIPS

1

July 1944
The Burden of a Transport Mission

"All engines ahead, one third. . . ."

"All engines stop."

In the stillness of the bridge, the captain's voice sounded with authority. It was July 1944, and the HIJMS *Natori* was moving very gently toward the quay of Palau Island, one of the western islands in the Caroline Islands. His body thrust forward from his perch on the forecastle, a sailor heaved a lead, which is a weight attached to a line. When tossed over the side of a ship, it enables one to determine the depth of the water or the movement of the ship through the water.

"She is moving forward, very slowly, sir. . . ."

The sailor reported the forward motion of the ship in such a slow tone that those in the strained environment on the bridge almost felt the movement of the ship.

"All engines back, one third. . . ."

"All engines stop."

The huge light cruiser, a ship of fifty-five hundred tons, stopped at the designated place alongside the quay. Commanded by Capt. Toshi Kubota, an outstanding line officer with years of experience with destroyers, the *Natori* was submissive, like a horse ridden by a capable jockey. The officer of the deck passed the word.

"Lookouts, antiaircraft gunners, take up your battle stations. All remaining hands begin off-loading the supplies. Bear a hand!"

The possibility of an air raid when the ship was alongside the quay was of great concern, for under these circumstances it would be impossible to maneuver to avoid being hit by bombs or torpedoes. An air strike would destroy the precious supplies that had been transported at great danger by the *Natori* and her crew. The time alongside the quay, therefore, had to be as short as possible. For this reason, the executive officer, Lt. Comdr. Isao Miyamoto, had already assigned working stations to the crew members, so that all the supplies, which had taken three days to load, could be off-loaded in two hours. The first lieutenant, Lt. (jg) Kentaro Nakajima, walked about the main deck with a baton as he supervised the off-loading operations.

The war in this area had become so intense that supplies could no longer be transported by low-speed vessels. Therefore, the *Natori*, which could sustain a speed of twenty-six knots, was now completing its third transport mission to Palau Island in the past two months. Crew members nicknamed their ship "The Natori Express," and their skill in loading and off-loading supplies compared with that of any professional express company.

For fear that the costly supplies would be destroyed by an air raid, the shore parties utilized all available trucks to carry supplies away from the quay to safe places. The *Natori*'s crew and shore parties worked with one accord, and the off-loading work was quickly completed.

Vice Adm. Kenzo Itoh, the commandant of the 30th Naval Base in Palau, came to the quay to meet with us as usual. The captain spoke to him from the bridge.

"Because there may be an air raid, please excuse me for greeting you from the bridge, Commandant. We are very grateful to you for coming all the way to see us, sir."

"Captain, thank you for your troubles in undertaking this death-defying transport to this island. Through your efforts our fighting strength has increased considerably. Incidentally, did you experience any enemy submarine attacks on your way over?"

"It's very thoughtful of you to ask, Admiral. Fortunately, not this time, sir."

"Glad to hear that. I wish you and your ship the best of luck."

"Same to you, sir. Now I must attend to duty. Please excuse me."

When Admiral Itoh commanded the 14th Destroyer Squadron, I was communications officer aboard his flagship, the *Naka*. I requested permission of the navigator, Lieutenant Kobayashi, to leave the ship, and with his approval went to greet the admiral.

4

"Commandant, communications officer Lieutenant Matsunaga, sir. It's good to see you again."

"I am sorry that you must make so many trips back and forth," said the admiral. "How have you been?"

"Fine, thank you, sir. How is your rheumatism?"

"Thank you. Because it's warm here, it does not bother me much these days on shore duty. By the way, I presume the *Natori* may come to anchor in Manila one of these days. My son-in-law works at the embassy there. His name is Koichi Takagi, and he is the first secretary. If you have time, please drop by to tell him Itoh is in good shape."

"Aye aye, sir. I will surely see him when I have the chance. Please excuse me now, Commandant."

After saying good-bye to the admiral, I walked down the main deck. On the quarter deck, many families were bidding farewell in tears. Women and children were required to evacuate Palau, but the men were to remain on the island and join the local voluntary army.

Often the words were spoken with tears and muffled by a handkerchief. But the boys were running merrily about the deck for the joy of being aboard a warship, which made their parents even sadder.

At the onset of the Pacific War, when the navy gained glorious victories at Hawaii and off the coast of Malaya, the entire nation was grateful to the navy. Undergoing the sorrow of parting from dear ones, what did these families think of the navy now? To avoid bringing them further grief, I realized that we had to transport them safely to Davao, on Mindanao Island in the Philippines. Besides the women and children the passengers included some navy pilots, army officers, and soldiers. The *Natori* was so crowded with passengers that we could hardly walk about inside the ship.

Returning to the bridge, I found the captain was already preparing to put to sea. Soon he passed the word.

"Stand by to put to sea. Take in all lines."

"Left rudder. Port back, one-third."

The *Natori* made a pivoted turnabout, and picked up a new heading. We were grateful that we did not encounter an air raid when the ship lay alongside the quay at Palau.

Palau Island lies in a vast atoll. It takes about two hours for a vessel to go from the quay of the island, through Kossol Passage, to the atoll's north entrance. Many hazardous reefs in these waters prohibit a vessel from passing through the passage at night. Ships on a transport mission to Palau, therefore, must enter the passage early in the morning, and clear the passage to the open sea by sundown. Enemy submarines knew this, and waited eagerly for their prey in these waters.

A scout-observation seaplane flew over the *Natori* to patrol and guard us from above. For safety, at least three planes were desirable, but this was too much to ask for under the circumstances. After completing its patrol mission, the plane circled over the *Natori*, rocking its wings as though to share with us the joy of uneventfulness. The *Natori's* crew, as well as the passengers, waved a farewell to the plane, soon out of sight as it headed toward the island.

Even after sundown, the *Natori* continued zigzag maneuvers while traveling at twenty-six knots, disguising her course to enemy submarines, as she headed for the harbor at Davao on Mindanao Island.

2
July 1944
Preparing for a Patrol Mission

As the USS *Hardhead* approached Oahu, those on deck caught their first sight of Diamond Head, the striking mountain formation that has greeted countless visitors to the Hawaiian Islands. It was July 5, 1944, and the *Hardhead* was completing an uneventful, eighteen-day passage from the Panama Canal to Pearl Harbor.

For most of us on board this new fleet submarine, it was our first visit to the Hawaiian Islands. Although we would be here for a few weeks, this was not a vacation. Instead, it was a time to complete our training and to make the preparations necessary to depart on our first war patrol.

These three weeks were a very busy time. During the first two weeks we went to sea early each morning and engaged in extensive training all day. This involved making a variety of simulated attacks on a destroyer that played the enemy. Sometimes we fired torpedoes, which had water ballast instead of a warhead, and were set to run deep so that they would pass under the target. What a welcome word it was when the target vessel reported that the torpedo had passed under the ship. Frequently these exercises extended through most of the night so that we could gain skill in making night attacks. This training was of vital importance, for most of us were newcomers to the navy and to submarine warfare.

Our commanding officer, Lt. Comdr. Fitzhugh McMaster, had

considerable submarine experience including command of an S–boat, an older type submarine used to patrol areas east and west of the Panama Canal, but this was his first command of a fleet submarine in the Pacific. However, four of the officers and all of the chief petty officers had extensive submarine experience, each having completed several war patrols. These men were important in training those of us who were novices. Even though we had all been trained at the submarine school in New London, Connecticut, it was a different experience to assume the responsibility for every facet of the operation of a submarine and develop the coordination and confidence needed to attack enemy ships.

As an ensign in the Naval Reserve, with very limited prior sea duty, I was certainly among those who needed this training. It was exciting and rewarding to gain the experience the other crew members and I needed as we prepared for our first war patrol.

During our days on Oahu there was one diversion I enjoyed immensely . While in port, each submarine was assigned a car. The captain had first priority on its use, but Captain McMaster rarely chose to exercise this prerogative. The next priority went to our second in command, the executive officer, Lt. Comdr. Charles McCall, a veteran submariner who had already completed six war patrols and knew the island well. He frequently collected two or three other officers to enjoy some sight–seeing and a dinner at one of the fine eating places on the island. Occasionally we took advantage of one of the best bargains available–a night at the Royal Hawaiian Hotel for one dollar. This was possible because the navy had taken over the hotel, making it available to transient navy personnel. What a great treat this was compared with sleeping on board! The only drawback was the need to be on board by 0630 to be ready for the activities of the day.

The last few days before our departure were spent making all the preparations needed for our first war patrol. These included loading twenty-four torpedoes, ammunition for our four–inch deck gun and our two Oerlikan antiaircraft guns, enough food to feed eighty–five men for seventy days, and 119,000 gallons of diesel fuel, enough to travel fourteen thousand miles.

We experienced one frustration in these last days in port, while busy loading these supplies. Many units on the base that we depended on for services or supplies sharply curtailed their work to prepare for Pres. Franklin D. Roosevelt's visit to Pearl Harbor. We recognized the importance of his meeting with the commanders of the U.S. forces in the Pacific and the boost his visit gave to the morale of the U.S. forces. But we found it frustrating to be hindered in our efforts to complete, on a tight time schedule, all we needed to do before our departure.

On July 26 the *Hardhead* departed Pearl Harbor on her first war patrol. A spirit of anticipation and adventure permeated the ship as we left Pearl Harbor, but it was tempered by our realization that making war patrols was a dangerous business. Almost every month one or more submarines did not return from their missions.

PART TWO

BACKGROUND AND REFLECTIONS

3

July 1944
Civilian Passengers on the Warship

When it became necessary to evacuate civilians by a warship, the busiest crew member was the first lieutenant, who was responsible for their well-being. In war time the number of crew members was increased, and as a consequence their living quarters were fully occupied. It was necessary, therefore, to accommodate these civilian passengers in storage rooms or passageways where there were many metal projections and a lot of gear was stored, and children could easily hurt themselves. As a result the first lieutenant gave constant attention to the safety of these passengers.

Among the crew members who were compelled to work with little rest and sleep were the cooks. Because of the limited capacity of the ship's galley, and having more than a thousand people on board, they had to prepare the same meal three times to serve everyone. When the ship was under way almost all the bulkhead doors were closed, leaving little opportunity for steam and heat to escape from the galley. Under these hot and humid conditions, the cooks, who stood for long periods as they prepared meals, became exhausted. Because not enough cooks were on board to work in shifts, they simply encouraged one another and worked hard to accomplish their tasks.

The medical department was also heavily involved in the care of passengers. Because people were packed in places not designed as living quarters and there was inadequate ventilation for the warm weather, many passengers developed a fever or became sea-sick. We were especially concerned about infections, for in these circumstances the disease could spread quickly to the crew members and passengers. If enough crew members became ill, the fighting strength of the ship would certainly be diminished. Therefore, hospital corpsmen were always on duty, closely watching the physical condition of the passengers.

On one occasion, the corpsmen on duty were notified that a passenger was very sick. Surgeon Lieutenant Yoshimura ran to where several women passengers were looking after a young woman suffering severe pain. He was then told she had gone into labor. Although he was an experienced medical corps officer, he had little experience in obstetrics. He passed the word to take her to the sick bay on a stretcher and a professional midwife among the passengers volunteered to assist. Fortunately, she had an easy delivery.

This kind of event was unexpected, for arrangements had been made with the authorities of the island that pregnant women would not be included in the passenger list. But, in the bustle of boarding, the condition of this passenger had been overlooked. Now it was more important to properly look after the newborn baby than to inquire why the woman had been allowed to board the ship.

About 2200, Lieutenant Nakajima, the first lieutenant, came up to the bridge to report the incident to the captain.

"Captain, a baby boy has just been born on the ship. The mother is a tofu vendor from Tokyo. Her husband is in the local voluntary army on the island. She respectfully asks you to be the boy's godfather."

The *Natori* was then under way in the darkness of the night under alert conditions. Peering ahead, the captain replied. "Well, I'm glad all went well. And now you want me to suggest a good name. Okay, the *Natori* is now under way in the Pacific Ocean [*Tai-hei-yo*]. From this I will take the word *yo* [meaning ocean], add the suffix *ichi* [which means the first, and is frequently used in Japanese boys' names], and give him the name Yoichi. Mr. Nakajima, send a bottle of wine to the mother in my name."

"Aye aye, sir. Thank you, sir."

The captain spoke in an unusually familiar tone to the navigator.

"Mr. Kobayashi, I don't suppose that captains of merchant ships have many occasions to become a godfather, much less captains of warships. In the eighty years of history of the Japanese Navy, I have never heard of a navy captain becoming a godfather, and that of a boy. I feel he is my rebirth."

"This is the first time I have ever heard of a baby born on a warship, Captain," the navigator replied.

Captain Kubota, from Nagano prefecture, was never hard to get along with, but usually he was not talkative, especially on the bridge, and had an inaccessible atmosphere about him. Yet he must have been pleased with the birth of Yoichi, for that night he was as merry as a cricket.

For breakfast the next morning the cooks prepared festive red rice (rice boiled with red beans), the typical Japanese food for celebrating a special occasion. The first lieutenant made an announcement over the public address system.

"Last night a baby boy was born on the ship. At the request of his mother, the captain agreed to be his godfather, and gave him the name Yoichi. Festive red rice is being served for breakfast to commemorate Yoichi's birth. Let us celebrate his happy birthday!"

Those on duty in the bridge sensed that all hands shared in this joy. The crew members, fatigued from strain and overwork, and the tired passengers, unaccustomed to a voyage on a warship, all celebrated this happy news.

When I was born my father was away from home, serving on a Japanese destroyer in the Mediterranean. (During World War I, Japan, as a member of the Allies, dispatched some destroyers to the Mediterranean Sea to assist in the battle against German U-boats.) Thus I took a special interest in Yoichi, for he was also born when his father was not present.

The rest of the journey was uneventful, and at 1300 on the following afternoon the *Natori* dropped anchors in the harbor at Davao, thus completing her important mission. The passengers eagerly awaited the landing craft, which shuttled them from the ship to the quay. The crew members and passengers had developed a sense of solidarity, for they had crossed the dangerous waters together and celebrated the birth of Yoichi. Waving their hands to bid farewell to one another, it seemed as though they were reluctant to part.

Looking at this scene, I recalled a line from "The Song of Men Advancing Southward.": "As you are a warrior with a sword, so I am a pioneer of the south."

In 1937, when I enrolled in the Naval Academy, a high school friend, Nakamura, sang this song for me as a farewell gift. Shortly after, he set out on a journey south to Micronesia, where he joined his uncle who lived there. Among these passengers there might be some who had left the Japanese homeland with hope of a better future in a distant land, just as Nakamura did. And now they had undergone the sorrow of parting from dear ones they had left behind. Their dreams were gone.

I remembered an event during our previous transport of civilians from Davao to Manila. A three-month–old baby developed a severe fever; despite careful nursing by the Surgeon Lieutenant Yoshimura, the baby died. The young mother begged to have the baby cremated after our arrival in Manila. Though we could not find it in our heart to bury the baby at sea, we could not allow her to keep the corpse in the narrow ship for a few more days. The executive officer persuaded her so graciously and sincerely that she finally consented to allow a burial at sea on the following morning.

For a burial at sea, the ship's carpenter makes a wooden coffin in such a way that it sinks into the sea. When a person serving in the military dies at sea, the coffin is covered with an ensign and dropped into the sea from the stern. Because the baby was a civilian, the national flag covered his coffin instead of an ensign.

At 0800 on the following morning, the bugle sounded attention and "the pillars of the country" was played solemnly. Many passengers and crew members quietly watched the ceremony in a dignified way as the coffin was dropped into the sea. Despite herself, the mother leaned forward and had to be restrained by nearby passengers. The *Natori* was cruising at high speed, her long white wake trailing from the stern. In my imagination, it appeared that the coffin was running after the ship. But soon it was out of sight, and the ensign flying at half mast continued to remind us of our sorrow.

4

July 1944
A White String Tied
around the Third Finger

In May and June the *Natori* had experienced slight water leak-age near the forward magazine. This had suddenly increased dur-ing the last trip from the Palaus, and the decision was made to dock her in Manila Bay. The dry dock we used, one of the largest in the Far East, had been built for the U. S. Navy, but was confiscated by the Japanese Navy after the war broke out. One day while she was in dock, I received permission from the executive officer to leave the ship to visit First Secretary Koichi Takagi at the Japanese Embassy, the son-in-law of Admiral Itoh in Palau. Thus I could keep the promise I had made to him.

Secretary Takagi proposed to take me to a Chinese restaurant on the north bank, an area where a tourist would not casually go. I was grateful for his kindness, but concerned when he said, "Even downtown Manila is now infested with guerrillas, and some Japanese have been killed. I will look ahead. Mr. Matsunaga, please keep a lookout behind us."

Both the Japanese Army Headquarters in the Philippines and the Philippine Area Fleet Headquarters of the navy were in Manila. If they could not keep order in Manila, the stronghold of the Japanese military forces in this region, how could they maintain peace and order in the other parts of the islands? Further, I had been told that the exchange rate of the Japanese military notes was dropping day by day. I was very much concerned about the situa-tion.

During dinner we avoided conversation about military matters, and talked mainly about personal matters. I learned that Mrs. Takagi had recently given birth to a boy in Tokyo. Just before bidding farewell to Mr. Takagi, he showed me a picture of the baby and said, "This baby is the first grandson of Commandant Itoh. Because the baby's grandfather is serving in the southern islands, we named the baby Namio, which means south sea man. Because they have discontinued mail service to Palau, I cannot send this picture to him. Mr. Matsunaga, may I entrust this picture to you?"

"I don't know what mission my ship will be assigned. But if I have the chance, I will deliver it to him. On that condition, I will keep it and carefully guard it," I said.

We decided to leave the restaurant early, certain that the route back would become more dangerous as the evening grew older. The popular horse-driven carriages known as *karatelas* were running, but I thought it safer to walk down the lighted boulevard as I made my way back to the pier on foot. Two months ago, when I strolled down the streets of Manila for the first time, *karatelas* were running very peacefully. But they seemed to be running hastily that night. Here and there I observed piles of sandbags, which suggested preparations for street fighting. Was all this real? Or was I being too imaginative?

As I walked down the boulevard, I reminisced about the days I had spent with the *Natori* since the first day I reported aboard. In January 1943, the *Natori* had been torpedoed by an enemy submarine off the coast of Ambon, Seram Island (near New Guinea) and the stern was badly damaged. The damage was further increased by near misses of bombs from B-24s. The *Natori* then proceeded to Singapore, where makeshift repairs were made in the Seletar dock. These repairs restored her performance to such an extent that she was able to proceed to the Japanese homeland at eighteen knots.

It was decided to make full-scale major repairs on the *Natori* at the Maizuru Navy Yard. Because this would take considerable time, she was assigned to the reserve fleet, and all the ship's company were detached from her and assigned new duty stations.

When I reported aboard the *Natori* in April 1944, she had recently been manned by a new crew, and was about to shove off for the training area in the Japan Inland Sea. The *Natori*'s officers expressed their strong conviction that three months of training would be needed after her commissioning shakedown.

For a warship to be effective, it needs many seasoned personnel thoroughly familiar with the ship and how it functions. These men are important in bringing a ship's fighting strength back to standard after many replacements are assigned to it. Soon several of the recruits usually emerge as brave, capable seamen. They also make a vital difference in the morale and effectiveness of the crew.

As I looked over the *Natori's* crew, I realized that there were few seasoned veterans or outstanding recruits. To put it plainly, I found few crew members of exceptional strength, and there was little to choose from.

Nearly thirty percent of the men assigned to my communications department were mere boys. As I greeted a young sailor sitting next to me, he replied respectfully, "Seaman Second Class Torao Watanabe, sir. Two months ago I completed the general course at the Communications School and was assigned directly to this ship. I am seventeen years old, sir."

As a warship of the Combined Fleet, the *Natori* was manned with the standard number of crew members. But because they were so young, and their training so brief, we concluded that we needed at least three months of training in the Inland Sea for the *Natori* to attain the standard fighting strength.

However, the Fleet Headquarters in Manila ordered the *Natori* to proceed to Manila immediately, which meant giving up the national holiday for the emperor's birthday on April 29. The crew was greatly discouraged by this decision, for they had been looking forward to this holiday. Those who had dependents in Maizuru, our home port, were especially disappointed, because they looked forward to celebrating it with their families.

After only one month of training, we left the homeland for the front.

When the *Natori* arrived in Manila in early June, we were surprised that no blackout was in effect, even though it was enforced everywhere in the Japanese homeland. Why was there no blackout in Manila, the stronghold of the front? After we arrived, the first month was spent idly, without any mission. We had complied with the urgent request of the Fleet Headquarters and proceeded to Manila on the double. But then they put us on standby! At night, as I looked at the glittering lights of Manila from the *Natori's* deck, I had my doubts if the headquarters adequately recognized the serious situation of the war. Now, two months later, as I walked back to the pier from my dinner, I saw that things had changed. The blackout was enforced, and piles of sandbags were everywhere. One could sense that at last serious preparations were being made in Manila.

We did not know when we would be dispatched to Palau Island, and then we would be alongside the quay for only two hours. I wondered, would I have time to deliver the photograph to Commandant Itoh? As a reminder to do this, I tied a white piece of string around the third finger of my left hand, resolving to keep the promise I had made to First Secretary Takagi.

5

July 27–31
En Route to Our Patrol Area

The *Hardhead* left Pearl Harbor at 1330 on July 27, with PC 580 as an escort. An hour later we made a trim dive, a carefully executed dive a submarine makes after leaving port to ensure that the ballast in the various tanks is properly adjusted to compensate for the supplies and fuel taken on board. At 2015 we released the escort, and proceeded on two engines, steering a zigzag course to make it difficult for any enemy submarines to attack us.

Our route on leaving Pearl Harbor included a brief stop at Midway Island, which lies thirteen hundred miles northwest of the Hawaiian Islands. The purpose of this stop was to top off our fuel tanks to have enough fuel for the thirty days we were scheduled to spend in our patrol area, and the subsequent journey to Fremantle, West Australia, which was to be our home port.

There were many reminders on board that we were now on our first mission. The forward torpedo room had torpedoes in each of its six tubes, and ten more stored in the room. This space had been designed so that the bunks of those quartered in this room were literally on top of and around the torpedoes.

The after torpedo room was similar in design but smaller. Its four torpedo tubes each carried a torpedo, and four torpedoes were stored in this compartment.

In these circumstances I reflected on how I became involved in this unique and potentially dangerous experience. During the

1941–42 academic year I was a senior mechanical engineering student at the University of Michigan, and made plans to take a position in industry after our June graduation.

But the events of December 7, 1941, when the Japanese bombed Pearl Harbor and the United States entered World War II, radically changed the plans of the nation and many persons. Spring vacation was canceled that year, the semester shortened, and graduation moved up to May 30.

During the spring I accepted a position in the Industrial Engineering Division of DuPont and began my work soon after graduation. But as the events of the war unfolded during the fall of 1942, particularly in North Africa and the Pacific, I grew restless in my work and concluded that I should join the V–7 program of the navy, which gave college graduates a four–month midshipmen school experience, designed to resemble the regular Naval Academy program, and then commissioned the graduates as ensigns.

I began midshipmen school in February 1943, on the *Prairie State* in New York City. This was the old battleship USS *Illinois*, with its engines and armament removed, and an arklike superstructure built over the deck. It was moored to a pier in the Hudson River at 137th Street. Our class was distinct from the rest of the V–7 program at Columbia University because all the midshipmen on the *Prairie State* were graduates of engineering programs, whereas most of the midshipmen on the campus of Columbia were liberal arts graduates. We felt discriminated against, not only because of the crowded living conditions on the *Prairie State*, as compared with dormitory living on the Columbia campus, but also because we had to march from 137th Street to Columbia University, at 116th Street, for a parade each Saturday morning and to Riverside Church for a Sunday evening service. (I managed to avoid the latter march by joining the choir, which traveled by bus for an early rehearsal.) The inconveniences of living on the *Prairie State*, however, were more than offset by a great spirit of camaraderie among us midshipmen.

As graduation from midshipmen school neared, we began thinking about what our next assignment might be. It was rumored that many would be assigned to further training at a radar or diesel school. My desire was sea duty, however, preferably on a smaller ship. We had no say in what our assignment would be, except that *Prairie State* graduates (because they were engineers) could volunteer for submarine duty. I volunteered for this duty because this was the only way I could be sure that I would achieve my goal of going to sea. After some physical and psychological tests, I was accepted.

Midshipmen school was organized alphabetically into companies, and it was through this arrangement that I came to know Gordon Taft. We had many common interests, including a commitment to the Christian faith, and we developed a close friendship. Because of this, I was delighted that he also volunteered for submarine duty. During our interviews we were asked if we wanted to go to San Diego, Key West, or New London. We were a bit dismayed to learn later that Taft had asked for San Diego while I asked for New London. But the navy resolved this problem by assigning us both to Key West!

At Key West there was a school to train navy personnel in sonar, the system by which one can detect and track enemy submarines. To make the training realistic, half a dozen old World War I submarines, called R–boats, would go to sea each morning and spend the day submerged, while those on training ships practiced detecting them with sound gear. It was decided that some of the newly commissioned ensigns who volunteered for submarine duty could gain practical experience in seamanship and in handling submarines by going to sea each day on these R–boats. We did this for three months and I found it to be excellent training. During this period Taft and I were roommates in the bachelor officers' quarters on the base.

One event during this duty stands out in my memory. Shortly before I arrived in Key West in late June, one of these boats, the R–12, had an accident and sank. On July 4, 1943, our submarine, the R–14, was assigned to carry out a special ceremony, which was to transport a large floral wreath on its deck, make a dive over the point where the R–12 had sunk, and leave the wreath floating in the sea. It was a poignant reminder that submarine duty can be dangerous, even in the absence of enemy action.

After three months in Key West our entire group was sent, in September, to the submarine school at New London for three months of training in an excellent, well–run program. During this period, my friend Taft and I were again roommates in the fine bachelor officers' quarters on the base.

At the conclusion of eight weeks of training, the grades of the 250 officers enrolled in the program were posted, along with all the assignments available on submarines. The student with the highest grades had first choice, the others following on down the list. I ranked high enough to have reasonably good choices, and selected SS365, the USS *Hardhead*, under construction in Manitowoc, Wisconsin. (Incidentally, Taft chose SS364, the USS *Hammerhead*.)

The term in submarine school ended just before Christmas, 1943, and I was able to spend the holidays with my family. After the holidays the crew of the *Hardhead* assembled in New London for some training, then moved to Manitowoc, where construction of the *Hardhead* was nearing completion. In April we had an extensive shakedown period on Lake Michigan, after which the *Hardhead* was declared ready for sea duty.

We left Manitowoc on a mild spring evening in May, and arrived at Chicago early the next morning. Two tugboats, one pulling us forward and the other guiding our stern, towed us through downtown Chicago and on to Lockport, about forty miles west of the city.

There a floating dry dock, which had been designed specifically to transport submarines down the Illinois and Mississippi rivers to New Orleans, awaited us. On entering the dry dock, the boat was lifted completely out of the water. The dry dock was then secured to a large riverboat, which would push the dry dock and its submarine cargo to New Orleans. This mode of transportation was necessary because the river was too shallow to accommodate the draft of a submarine, and also because the great maneuverability of the riverboat was necessary to navigate the bends and turns in the rivers.

Because there were very few duties for the crew during this voyage, all those who were married were given six days' leave, with the stipulation that they join us in New Orleans. The only other unmarried officer besides myself was a very capable officer, Lt. Eugene Pridonoff, who had already completed six war patrols, and we joined the captain and about twenty crew members on a wonderful trip down the Mississippi. I found Mark Twain's *Life on the Mississippi* in the boat's library, and thoroughly enjoyed reading this while lounging on the deck of a submarine as it was traveling down the Mississippi River in a floating dry dock.

We arrived in New Orleans on schedule, where the rest of the crew joined us. We came out of the dry dock, took on supplies, and proceeded with the assistance of an experienced river pilot, to the mouth of the Mississippi. There the pilot left us and we proceeded on our own to the Panama Canal. We kept an especially sharp lookout during this period, steering a zigzag course because of reports that a German U–boat had been sighted in this area.

Our passage through the Panama Canal was a fascinating experience, as was our brief stay in Panama City. We spent the following week in the Perlas Islands off the west coast of Panama, where we worked all day and many nights with a destroyer, which acted as an enemy ship, to develop our skills in tracking and attacking target ships in a wide range of circumstances. Each officer and crew member had a specific battle station assignment during such attacks, and we worked hard to hone our personal skills and achieve a high level of coordination.

My assignment was plotting officer, which involved tracking the target ship using the captain's periscope observations, sonar data, and, when on the surface, radar data. I then reported to the captain my best estimate of the course and speed of the target and the optimum course and speed to intercept the target. This complemented the work of Lieutenant Pridonoff, who operated the Torpedo Data Computer, which performed such calculations automatically and set the gyroscopes in the torpedoes so that they would follow a course that would intersect the target. All these activities required tremendous coordination, and this training period in the Perlas Islands was of vital importance in preparing us for our future assignments.

It was with excitement and anticipation that we left Panama City in mid-June, en route to Pearl Harbor and the experiences that would follow.

6

August 1–12
On Patrol

"Clear the bridge."

As the officer of the deck (OOD) called out this order, he sounded two blasts on the diving alarm. Immediately, throughout the boat, those on duty in the various compartments performed the tasks needed to dive the submarine. In the control room, under the supervision of the diving officer, the chief petty officer on duty opened the vents that allowed the ballast tanks to flood, and closed the valve on the main ventilation system. The men in the diesel engine compartments quickly shut down the diesel engines. Those operating the electrical controllers in the maneuvering room switched the source of power for the electric motors driving the propellers from the diesel engine generators to the batteries.

Meanwhile the five lookouts on the bridge scrambled down the conning tower hatch; two of them manned the diving planes. The officer of the deck, after making sure that all hands were below, pulled down the hatch cover as he came below, and stepped aside while the quartermaster secured the watertight hatch cover. This all had to be done quickly, because the hatch would be under water in less than twenty-five seconds.

The chief petty officer and the diving officer were monitoring all these events on the "Christmas tree," an electrical display of lights that showed red when the hatches and vents into the boat were open and green when closed. When all the lights were green the diving officer would call for compressed air to be released into the boat. As he did so, he carefully watched the barometer, which would indicate an increase in pressure if the boat was airtight (which meant it was also watertight). As soon as it was evident that the boat was holding the increase in air pressure, the diving officer called out, "Secure the air. Pressure in the boat," indicating that the ship was ready for submerged operation.

This was a routine practice dive on our first full day out of Pearl Harbor. We continued these dives each day, along with many other drills, as we proceeded to the patrol area. Through the extensive training of the past two months, we had gained much skill and coordination in all these exercises. We were confident that we were ready to perform under combat conditions.

We arrived at Midway Island at 1000 on July 31 and remained there for five hours while taking on fuel and making a few minor repairs. Two years earlier, in June 1942, the Battle of Midway, the first major naval battle of the war, had been fought in these waters. It had been an important turning point in favor of the United States. On departing Midway Island we proceeded on a zigzag course on two engines toward the area we were assigned to patrol, off Surigao Strait on the east coast of the Philippines.

The *Hardhead* was powered by four sixteen-cylinder diesel engines, each connected to an electric generator. The electricity from these generators powered the electric motors that drove our two propellers, supplied the entire electrical system, and charged the large, multicelled batteries that provided power when we were submerged. While on the surface we normally used two engines operating at about eighty percent capacity. This gave us a speed of twelve knots and good fuel economy. With all engines operating at capacity we could achieve our flank speed of twenty knots.

When submerged we normally cruised at three knots. The batteries, when fully charged, could sustain this speed for twenty-four hours. Our top speed submerged was eight knots, but at this speed the battery would be fully discharged in one hour.

The projected length of our patrol (sixty days) and the distance we might travel made it important to be economical with diesel fuel. And because we might, at any time, have to operate submerged for an extended period, we tried to keep the battery fully charged at all times. Therefore, when we surfaced after being submerged for an extended period, we immediately began to recharge the batteries.

On August 11, shortly before entering this patrol area, we

encountered a major typhoon, and experienced winds of fifty to sixty knots and waves of twenty-five feet. The seas were so violent that we had to close the main ventilation valve to prevent taking on water. This meant that the air for operating the diesel engines had to be drawn through the conning tower hatch and the compartments leading to the engine rooms. At the height of the storm the forward steel deck caved in and the lifelines on the deck were carried away. The final stages of this storm were to have a major impact on those who survived the sinking of the *Natori*.

The following day we entered our patrol area, and for the next three days we submerged at daybreak as we patrolled off Samar Island. We surfaced shortly after sunset and continued to patrol while recharging the batteries.

The crew was divided into three watches; each watch was on duty four hours and off eight. In addition, each crew member had specific assignments for battle stations submerged, battle stations surface, and when the deck guns were manned.

The *Hardhead* operated under the control of the commander of submarines of the Seventh Fleet, based in Australia. While at sea we maintained radio contact with the base, but to avoid detection by the enemy, submarines maintained radio silence except when they had something of vital importance to report. However, each evening the base transmitted messages to all submarines at sea, giving orders and information to each submarine, and transmitting back to the fleet any messages it had received from submarines. Because all messages were sent in code, each night one officer had the responsibility to decode these messages. In this way the captain and the officers of each submarine knew about all the activities taking place in the submarine fleet in the southwest Pacific, as well as receiving specific messages for their boat. Submarines operating farther north were under the control of the Pacific Fleet based in Hawaii.

One critical aspect of life on a submarine is the very limited amount of water available. We had two stills for making fresh water from salt water, but the capacity was limited to about five hundred gallons a day. The batteries required about two-thirds of this, leaving the rest for drinking, cooking, and bathing. There was no water for showers and laundry, and all bathing had to be done out of a small wash basin. Each crew member carried four to eight changes of clothes, and decided at what point in the eight- or nine-week patrol period to make each change!

As a reserve officer, I had very little introduction to celestial navigation during my brief midshipman school experience. But now I had the wonderful opportunity to spend at least two hours each night on the bridge, completely open to the night sky. By listening to those who knew the stars, making frequent use of a star chart, and carefully observing the stars, I learned the names and positions of many stars, and developed a deep appreciation for the beauty of the night sky. Soon I could estimate time and direction accurately simply by glancing at the sky. By watching the navigator and quartermaster in their work, I also learned how to take a star fix with a sextant, and from these observations and the use of the appropriate tables to determine our position. These days were a great learning experience and a time to appreciate the beauty of the heavens.

I have never forgotten the beauty of the sunsets in the tropics. The open bridge provided a wonderfully clear view of the sky and was a great place to observe the beauty of these sunsets. When serving as officer of the deck, however, my first and primary responsibility was to keep a careful watch and perform this duty to the best of my ability.

Because a submarine does not have a chaplain aboard, I took it upon myself to lead an informal worship service on Sundays at mid afternoon, one of the few times the main eating area was not being used to serve meals. The service consisted primarily of a short reading and study from the Bible, followed by some prayers. This was a meaningful experience for those of us who sought, even in these unusual circumstances, to remember who we were and reflect our Christian faith in our attitudes, performance, and relationships.

As we continued our patrol activities, we wondered when our first encounter with the enemy would come. We were eager for an encounter. This was why we had undergone these months of rigorous training, why we were here, far from home and from our normal activities. Behind this commitment was the conviction that this was right for us and for our country.

PART THREE

THE ENCOUNTER

7

August 1–9
Difficult Circumstances
for an Important Mission

In June and July of 1944, the superior U.S. forces invaded and captured Saipan, Guam, and Tinian in the Mariana Islands. The Japanese forces defending these islands fought gallantly, although they had no expectation of receiving reinforcements and supplies. By late July mopping operations on these islands by the U.S. forces was well under way.

To cope with the worsening situation, the Japanese Navy decided to prepare for the anticipated invasion of the Philippine Islands. As the first step reinforcements were sent to the Palaus, where a preliminary skirmish was likely to take place. During June and July the *Natori* made three trips to Palau with urgently needed supplies.

In August, as the *Natori* left the dry dock after her repairs in Manila, Vice Adm. Arata Oka, the commander in chief of the Philippine Area Fleet, eagerly awaiting the availability of the *Natori*, sent the following action dispatch:

> *Natori* and No. 3 Armed Transport shall engage in transport of urgently needed supplies and equipment to Palau. Shove off from Manila at 0900 August 10 and arrive at Kossol Passage in the Palaus at 1030 August 13. *Natori* shall accommodate as many evacuees from the island as possible and then

return to Manila. For No. 3 Armed Transport, expect further action dispatch at a later date.

Upon receipt of this dispatch, the *Natori* began loading supplies and boarding passengers, including eight reserve ensigns from universities. Among the other passengers were sixty PT boat crew members. Because of the rapidly deteriorating situation of the war, and also the waxing of the moon (we wanted to avoid travel in moonlight), this was considered the last opportunity to reinforce the Palaus. Both the passengers and crew were aware of the increasingly difficult circumstances.

To increase her loading capacity, the *Natori* had received an advisory from the Fleet Headquarters to off-load the lifeboats. The *Natori* had three launches fitted with engines, and three lifeboats fitted with oars. The captain flatly turned down this advisory, asserting that it was entirely up to the commanding officer to make the final decision about off-loading the lifeboats, and not a decision to be made by Headquarters. He was, however, fully aware of the intentions of Headquarters, and in lieu of the boats, he decided to off-load the spare torpedoes. Lt. Choji Murano, the torpedo officer, was strongly opposed to the captain's decision, and objected at the risk of his position. Torpedoes require careful attention from the crew members of the torpedo department, who tend to treat them as their children, so it was quite natural for the torpedo officer to take a stand against the captain.

The captain was firm but understanding.

"I have served on destroyers for a number of years and I know very well how you feel about off-loading the spare torpedoes, and why you take a position against me, Mr. Murano," he stated. "But you must realize the deteriorating situation from a broad perspective, and disregard your personal feelings as torpedo officer. I want you to obey my decision."

"Aye aye, Captain," he replied. The spare torpedoes were promptly off-loaded from the *Natori*.

Because the *Natori* was to carry many passengers, the captain ordered that lumber be loaded on the deck, and tied down with manila ropes in such a manner that it would break loose easily and float in the sea if the ship should sink. This lumber would then be available as makeshift rafts to those who abandon ship.

The *Natori* was a relatively old ship, having been in commission for twenty-three years. However, the ship's company had great pride in the ship and was prepared to fight gallantly, even if this meant their own death, when the time came for the United States and Japan to fight a decisive naval battle. Until now these transport missions were regarded as temporary tasks, and had been carried out with full armament and equipment on board. But off-loading the spare torpedoes was significant, for it meant that transporting supplies took the place of the primary mission for which the *Natori* was designed and commissioned. The crew felt like professional ball players who had been assigned to a scrub team, but in reality the ship's company would be exposed to more danger than ever before.

Before getting under way from Manila, Captain Kubota made arrangements with the commanding officer of the No. 3 Armed Transport, Lt. Comdr. Wataru Hamamoto, that if either of the ships was damaged during the voyage, the undamaged ship would forsake the damaged ship and her crew, and proceed on her mission to Palau.

This prearrangement between the two captains made this mission all the more dangerous, because no rescue by the consort could be expected when it was needed the most. The three prior missions to Palau had been stressful for the crew, though outwardly they remained calm and composed. But now the situation had deteriorated faster than the crew could handle, and smiles gradually disappeared from their faces.

The Philippines, with some seven thousand islands, stretch 1,150 miles from north to south and 680 miles from east to west. Its subtropical climate divides a year into two seasons: a rainy season from April through October and a dry season from November through March. As the *Natori* was engaged in this transport mission during the rainy season, she frequently encountered rainsqualls. When a rainsquall approached the ship the order was given:

"All hands at leisure, stand by for a rainsquall bath."

Because the warship had a limited supply of fresh water, we welcomed this "heaven gifted" water, as an old Japanese song goes. Naked crew members appeared from hatches, gathered on the main deck, and quickly soaped their bodies. Sometimes, contrary to their expectation, the rainsquall suddenly changed course and disappeared or consisted of a brief sprinkle. Then they found themselves in an embarrassing situation, and begged for a little water from the first lieutenant, which brought a hearty laugh from those watching the scene. These rainsqualls not only supplied water, but also brought laughter to the crew.

Because the ship held a large amount of ignitable materials, such as gunpowder and gasoline, there were places where smoking was not allowed at any time. There were, however, places designated as "tobacco trays," where enlisted men gathered for conversation and relaxation. Often groundless rumors emanated from these areas. Now rumor had it that after this transport mission to Palau was completed, the *Natori* would be dispatched to Singapore to bring supplies to Manila, where we would be given a two-week leave.

Because Manila was not an industrial city, many goods were imported from either Singapore or Hong Kong. Therefore, this rumor seemed quite reasonable, and the idea cheered the crew considerably.

With a mixture of many emotions and thoughts, the crew of the *Natori* prepared for her fourth transport mission to Palau.

8

August 18
Torpedoed

The *Natori* and the No. 3 Armed Transport shoved off from Manila on August 10 as scheduled. On the following day we were approaching the east exit of Surigao Strait when we received an action dispatch from the commander in chief, the Philippine Area Fleet: "Strong probability of enemy task force off the east coast of the Philippines. Discontinue mission and return."

We diverted to Cebu Island and set off again at 0800 on August 13, but once again returned to Cebu to stand by after being informed that an enemy task force had been sighted. Out of concern for their health and well-being, the crew was divided into two groups, and each was given two hours of shore leave to explore the island.

Cebu is rich in history. Magellan visited there in 1521, after a three-month journey from the straits at the southern tip of South America that now bear his name. Beginning in 1565, Legaspi made Cebu a stronghold of Spanish colonial power, religion, and culture. Now it is filled with historic ruins of churches, crosses, and fortresses, and its university dates from this period. It is not a large island, but Cebu's harbor has a pier large enough to accommodate ships of seven thousand tons.

While on Cebu, Paymaster Lt. Dairoku Imai bought a supply of mangoes, the queen of fruits, and each crew member was given three mangoes. I lost no time in eating all three of mine, but most crew members ate just one and kept the other two to enjoy later. Little did they know that the opportunity to eat the mangoes would soon pass.

Though it was important to consider enemy ship movements in deciding when to depart, we could not, because of the waxing moon, delay any longer. At 0700 on August 16, we shoved off from Cebu for the third time, but this time we headed north through the inland waters for San Bernadino Strait, which lies some 150 miles north of Surigao Strait, and nested in the anchorage west of San Bernadino Strait that evening. At 0700 on the following morning, August 17, we weighed anchors, and proceeded eastward through the strait at flank speed, into the open sea.

Soon after we cleared the strait, a large enemy plane began keeping contact with us, while remaining out of range of our anti-aircraft (AA) guns. We suspected that this plane was sending reports on us to his base, but we had no means to chase him away. The distance to the Marianas, where U.S. planes were based, was about seven hundred miles, which meant we could experience an air raid late in the afternoon. To disguise our destination, we changed course to the north for a while and then headed east. Fortunately the sun set without our having had an attack from the air.

We received information that a friendly patrol plane had sighted a surfaced enemy submarine at 096°, 466 miles from Manila at 1100 on August 15. To avoid encountering this submarine, the *Natori* unit changed course so as to pass 100 miles south of that point at 0000 on the morning of August 18. (Note: the submarine sighted was not the *Hardhead*.)

That night we monitored the frequencies used for transmission to and from enemy submarines, and found much radio traffic. We could not break their coded dispatches, but presumed that several enemy submarines were nearby. I was responsible for communications intelligence, and reported this to the bridge. Because the enemy plane had been in contact with us during the daytime, and many transmissions involved enemy submarines, we kept a strict watch.

About 2300 on August 16, the officer decoding the radio transmissions to the *Hardhead* brought the captain a top secret message that had just been received, informing us of the movement of some unidentified Japanese ships, and giving their locations at various times over the next two days. We were aware that such top secret messages, giving precise data on the movement of enemy ships, were frequently sent to submarines, and concluded that most likely this information was gained by breaking the Japanese code. For this reason the messages were classified top secret. Only the captain and the officers were aware of these messages, and we carefully avoided any hint of them in our conversations with the crew or when we were off the ship.

On receiving this message Captain McMaster and Executive Officer McCall, who also served as navigator, plotted the indicated course of these ships, determining that if we traveled at near full speed for the next nineteen hours, we could intercept these ships some three hundred miles east of the Philippines. We set out immediately on this course, traveling through rough seas and an overcast sky throughout the day. At sunset, as Lieutenant Commander McCall was trying to get his evening star fix, the clouds parted just enough for sextant observations on three stars. This was important, for it enabled us to determine our position with accuracy. We hoped that the enemy ships could also get a star fix, so that they could follow their assigned course.

By 1930 on August 17 we were on the reported path of these ships, about five hours before the target was scheduled to arrive. We made a trim dive so that the boat would be properly ballasted for good underwater maneuverability.

If the target appeared at the anticipated time, shortly after midnight, the moon would already have set, and with the heavy overcast, it would be a very dark night, making a surface attack feasible. With this in mind, we partly flooded some of the ballast tanks so that we rode lower in the water, thereby presenting a smaller silhouette, which would make the boat harder to detect.

If the enemy ships were on the course indicated in the top secret dispatch, they would be detected in the west, traveling almost due east at high speed. Therefore, on surfacing from the trim dive we began to cruise back and forth slowly across the projected course of the target while maintaining a careful radar watch, particularly to the west.

Just before 0100 we had a radar contact in the west at a range of 22,000 yards. We immediately went to flank speed in an easterly direction, the same course the target was on. In this way we could maintain a position ahead of the target while taking bearings and ranges on the target, to determine its course and speed. Lieutenant

Pridonoff on the Torpedo Data Computer and I on the plotting table were responsible for these calculations. After about fifteen minutes, we slowed our speed slightly so that the target would gradually come closer. When the range was 16,000 yards, radar detected a second smaller ship on the starboard quarter of the larger ship we had first detected.

By this time we had determined that the target was on a base course of 085°, was zigging 30° every five minutes, from course 070° to 100°, and the speed was seventeen knots. We decided that the larger ship was our primary target.

At 0219, the range was 12,000 yards, and we turned toward the target to prepare for a bow shot on the port side of the target. By using this approach, the second smaller ship would be on the far side of the target, thus leaving the port side of the target free for our approach. When the range was 8,000 yards, the captain and those on the bridge could see the target through their binoculars. From this point on, the bearing of the target was taken from visual observations on the bridge by Lt. John Bragg, through the binoculars on the bridge gyroscopic repeater, which transmitted the bearing of the target directly to the Torpedo Data Computer. As the target came closer, those on the bridge could see a large mast forward and one large stack, and believed it might be a battleship.

The captain decided that, because the night was so dark, we could make a surface attack. We realized, however, that because of the speed of the target, we would have only one opportunity to attack. If we missed, the target would simply outrun us. Therefore, the captain's strategy was to first fire the six bow tubes with our bow pointing toward the ship, slightly ahead of the target (like a hunter leading a fast flying duck). We would then make a sharp left turn at flank speed, so that the *Hardhead* was running parallel with the target, and, from this position, fire the four stern tubes, thus utilizing our maximum attacking power.

Even then a torpedo was a remarkable device. The conventional torpedo carried a tank of alcohol and high pressure air; the steam and gases generated by burning the alcohol with this air provided the power for propulsion. The stern tubes carried recently developed torpedoes that utilized batteries for propulsive power. These torpedoes had the advantage of being difficult to detect, for they had no exhaust gases, which made the track of a conventional torpedo visible. However, electric torpedoes were slower and had a shorter range.

Each torpedo was equipped with a gyroscope, which controlled a steering mechanism that kept the torpedo on a predetermined course determined by the Torpedo Data Computer. This information was continuously fed into the torpedo, so that the torpedo was ready for firing at all times. The torpedo was fired from the torpedo tube by a blast of compressed air, at which time the propulsion system was triggered, and the torpedo proceeded on the predetermined course. (One concern submarines always had was the possibility that the rudder on the torpedo would jam full right or left, causing the torpedo to make a circular run and come back and hit the vessel that fired. One of the United States submarines was sunk through such a mishap.) A torpedo is also set to run at a given depth; the larger the ship, the deeper the depth is set.

The crucial issue in scoring a hit is whether the course and speed of the target and the distance to the target have been determined correctly. To allow for inaccuracy in these estimates, and because the target may change course or speed at the last moment, a "spread" of torpedoes is fired. For example, if four torpedoes are fired, the gyroscopes are set so that one will pass ahead of the target, one will hit the forward part of the ship, another the after part, and the fourth will pass astern, in the hope that at least one will hit the target. Because the target was a large ship, Captain McMaster ordered that the depth on the torpedoes be set at ten feet.

At 0237, our bow pointed slightly ahead of the target, Lieutenant Bragg focusing the gyrocompass repeater on the target, and the *Hardhead* 3,500 yards at 60° off the port bow of the target, we fired our bow tubes at ten-second intervals. Because the target was still coming toward us, the actual torpedo run was 2,800 yards; it would take about two minutes for the torpedoes to reach the target. Our plan was to fire all six bow tubes, but the outer door on the number six tube would not open, so five torpedoes were on their way to the target.

At 0238, as soon as the last bow tube torpedo was fired, we went to flank speed and made a sharp left turn so that we were running parallel with the target. We were now only 2,200 hundred yards from the target. When this maneuver was completed at 0240, those on the bridge observed that a large dim green light on the mast of the target was lighted for about five seconds.* Forty seconds later, as we were running parallel with the target, we fired our four stern tubes. These tor-

---

*When Mr. Matsunaga met Captain McMaster in 1988, he told him that any tornado wakes by either ship were to be indicated to the consort with the dim light, green for starboard, red for port. Apparently those on the *Natori* saw wakes of torpedoes that had crossed their track, and thought the torpedoes had been fired from the starboard side.

pedoes had to turn 90° to the left to pick up the bearing for the correct approach to the target. This was a much more difficult operation than the straight-on bow tube shots we had just undertaken.

By this time the bow tube torpedoes had covered the distance to the target, and at least one hit should have been observed. But there were no hits, though in all the action and excitement, we focused on firing our stern tubes, not on listening for explosions. At 0243, two minutes after firing the stern tubes, we heard the first of several explosions. Lieutenant Pridonoff shouted in my ear, "A hit." As a veteran submariner, he knew what to expect, but for me this was a totally new experience.

After the second explosion those on the bridge saw two large simultaneous fires of about five seconds' duration just aft of the mainmast; the flames were shooting up to two-thirds the height of the mast. In the light of these flames, those on the bridge observed more of the structure of the ship, and were convinced that the target was a battleship. Shortly after this the target slowed and came to a stop. Later a lookout reported that he had seen an explosive flash on the far side of the target, and we concluded that this could have been a hit on the second ship. This ship milled around the target briefly, then headed toward us at ten knots, and at 0305 was detected heading due north at thirteen knots. We were now 8,000 yards from the target, which appeared to be dead in the water, and we began to reload the torpedo tubes.

Sometime after 0200, on the early morning of August 18, soon after coming out of a rainsquall, we observed a blue flare being shot up in the dark sky from the No. 3 Armed Transport. It indicated, according to the prearrangement between the ships, that a torpedo wake to starboard had been sighted. The OOD then shouted.

"Starboard lookout, can you see the torpedo wake?" In a little while he shouted back.

"Right 120 degrees, torpedo wake." On hearing this report, the OOD passed the word immediately.

"Right full rudder, bear a hand. All engines ahead, full!"

But before the ship responded to the OOD's engine and rudder order and made an accelerated turn, a torpedo hit the *Natori* with a deafening roar, and the hull vibrated violently from the explosion. The OOD passed the word, "All hands at battle stations."

The aft portion of the bridge caught on fire and instantaneously burst into flames higher than the ship's mast. The main generators must have been damaged by the explosion, for in an instant all electric–powered machines and equipment ceased to function. The bridge passed the word.

"Fire! The location of the fire is the forward lower radio room."

"Make it watertight! Damage in No. 2 fire room."

Manual pumps and fire–fighting equipment were all brought to the forward end of the ship. But the primitive damage control work we could accomplish under dim flashlights had little impact. The executive officer reported to the bridge that he was taking charge of the damage control party on the forward middle deck.

After this report, special service gunnery officer Lt. (jg) Sadaji Suzuki reported to the bridge "The forward and aft magazines are ready to flood and we are standing by ready to proceed."

We all were very much relieved to hear his report, because when a ship is damaged one of the most dreadful things that can happen is induced explosions in the magazines where ammunition is stored. As the gunnery crew flooded the magazines, we were grateful that we avoided this added difficulty.

I had the messenger, who was on the bridge, call the forward lower radio room on the speaking tube. Although he called many times, we had no response; instead, white smoke and a heavy odor were coming out of the tube. Apparently the four or five radiomen on duty in this compartment had been killed by the explosion.

The captain had an urgent first dispatch sent to the Fleet Headquarters in Manila: "0240 August 18. Torpedoed by enemy submarine. One hit. Lat 12° 05′ N. Lon 129° 26′ E. Despite serious damage, no fear of sinking at present. Unable to maneuver."

With the desperate, makeshift repair work carried out by the chief engineer, Engr. Lt. Comdr. Sadasuke Ishiguro and his men, enough steam was generated to enable us to get under way at low speed. The captain then ordered a second dispatch to be sent: "Getting under way westward, at six knots."

Executive Officer Miyamoto came up to the bridge to give a damage report to the captain. He said that although they were pumping water out of the forward lower deck with two manual pumps, and were also using mess containers passed from hand to hand, the leakage was much faster than could be removed. As the water level rose to knee height, they were forced to close the bulkhead doors to make it watertight. Also, the No. 2 fireroom appeared to be filled with water.

At 0330 all the torpedo tubes had been reloaded. While reloading we had tracked the escort vessel on its course due north until it disappeared from the radar screen at a range of 14,000 yards.

Captain McMaster then decided we should return to the target, which we assumed to be a battleship, and assess the situation. It was quite puzzling, for the battleship allowed us to close to within 2,200 yards without being detected, and did not shoot at us. Further, the escort vessel paid no attention to us, and simply left the scene, taking a northerly course. What kind of escort vessel was this?

At 0400 our radar detected the target at a range of 12,500 yards. As we proceeded toward the target we tracked it and found it was proceeding west on course 280° at a speed of one-half knot. At a range of 7,000 yards those on the bridge could see the target through their binoculars and again concluded it was a battleship. The captain decided that we would fire a second round of torpedoes from the bow tubes using a depth setting of six feet.

At 0441, with the target 3,500 yards away and traveling due west at very low speed, and its broadside directly ahead of us, and the *Hardhead* traveling slowly due south, we fired the six bow tubes.

After firing we proceeded due east at flank speed. Two and a half minutes later we heard a series of seven explosions, and those on the bridge observed six explosive flashes along the target's waterline.

After we determined that there would be no counterattack, we slowed our speed and began to circle around the target to the east, preparing to approach it from the south. Because it would soon be daylight, the captain decided to report the situation to the base by radio, so that if the target got away from us, land- or carrier-based planes could take up the attack.

While the *Natori* was getting under way westward with the makeshift repairs, at 0330, about fifty minutes after the first torpedo attack, the enemy submarine made an attack upon us for the second time. We clearly observed a torpedo dashing through the water toward the *Natori*, trailing white wakes behind. But at a speed of only six knots, we could not possibly execute a quick and effective evasion maneuver. The torpedo hit the *Natori* near her aft mast, and we were resigned to this being our last moment. The enemy submarine wanted to give the *Natori*, already badly damaged, the coup de grace. By good fortune, however, the torpedo failed to explode.

The damned enemy submarine! It would not leave us alone, even in the great difficulties we were experiencing. It was next to impossible to sight a periscope in the dark night, particularly in the rough open sea we were experiencing. And we could expect no help from our consort, for, to avoid a second disaster, the No. 3 Armed Transport had vanished out of sight to the north for a while.

The torpedo officer, Lieutenant Murano, and the special service morale officer, Ens. Kiyoji Maruyama, who had taken charge of the damage control party at the scene of leakage, came up to the upper deck. They were soaking wet and bleeding from wounds in their faces. From their reports it was clear that despite the men's utmost efforts there was no way to stay ahead of the leakage.

As the last countermeasure, the captain ordered that heavy objects be jettisoned to sustain the buoyancy of the ship. First, the main anchors, one on each side at the bow (one weighed four tons) were jettisoned. The equipment was next to go, along with supplies for the Palaus, which included sixteen aerial torpedoes, AA guns and ammunition, provisions, and other supplies. These were thrown overboard, one after another. Still, the bow of the *Natori* continued to droop bit by bit into the sea, like a person bowing his head far down, as the leakage continued to increase. Last of all, the captain passed the word to jettison all shells for 5.5" guns, except those stored close to the guns.

Leading seaman Yamamoto, the No. 1 gunner of the No. 1 main battery, was bidding farewell to the shells with tears in his eyes. Gunners become attached to these shells and are loath to part with them, for they experienced both pleasure and pain as they trained by day and by night to load the guns quickly. But if we were to save the *Natori*, jettisoning the shells was unavoidable; thus they were dropped overboard one after another.

About when Ens. Akio Hoshino, the assistant navigator, was determining the ship's position from observations of the sun at sunrise, the No. 3 Armed Transport neared us. The captain ordered that a visual signal be sent: "Disregard our ship and carry on as scheduled. Wish you success in accomplishing your mission, and best of luck. Peace be with you."

As the No. 3 Armed Transport circled around the *Natori* twice, it was clear that she was hesitant to leave us behind. Then she sent a visual back: "Will proceed to Palau as scheduled."

Soon the No. 3 Armed Transport was out of sight, and we were alone in desperate circumstances. None of the *Natori* crew members had regarded the consort as a rescue ship, nor did they expect assistance from her. But when it came down to it, we could not help feeling forsaken and abandoned, although no one spoke of it. It seemed she was turning a cold shoulder to us, even though this had been arranged in advance. It was all we could think about, for the *Natori* would soon be going down, sinking in waters three hundred miles away from the nearest shore.

At 0538 we proceeded on course 300° to approach the target again, and at 0554 the lookouts sighted it from the bridge. We began tracking it and found it was dead in the water. Those on the bridge had a better look at the target now, and concluded that it was a battleship with a tall Pagoda–type foremast, a single tall stack, and a fairly heavy mast toward the rear of the ship. I asked the captain for permission to come to the bridge for a quick look at the target, which he granted.   Just then the target began firing at us and the flashes and tracers were visible. Shortly after I went back to my station in the conning tower, we dove, for the captain had decided that we should begin a submerged approach at our normal submerged speed of three knots.

"Periscope, left ninety degrees, two zero (2000 meters)," the lookout shouted in a shrill voice. All of our earlier emotions vanished in a moment. After the sound of the bugle call "commence firing," the captain passed the word.

"Left ninety degrees, commence firing at enemy submarine."

At that instant, in response to the captain's orders, the 5″ AA guns and the 25 mm machine guns opened fire. As the AA guns roared, like a wounded animal roars with all its might, towers of white water rose one after another near the white crested wake made by the advancing periscope. The red lines of tracer machine gun bullets focused on the target. The periscope soon disappeared, but there was no knowing how much damage we had given the submarine. The *Natori* had to depend entirely on lookouts, for the sonars were not functioning because of the lack of electric power. We continued to concentrate all our attention on detecting the enemy submarine.

The long-awaited sunrise was drawing near. The eastern sky turned to pale and then to rose. The hours during which the enemy submarine continued to attack us would soon be over. Strangely, a relieved expression appeared on many faces. Our bombardment certainly had changed our emotions. It is said that even when damaged, offense is always the best defense. But we knew that the night battle would soon come to an end, and we were glad of it.

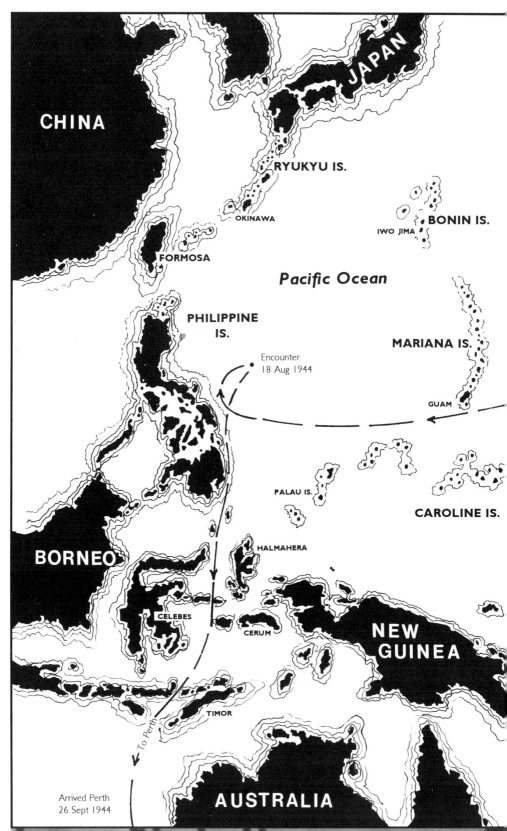

CHINA

JAPAN

RYUKYU IS.

OKINAWA

BONIN IS.

IWO JIMA

FORMOSA

Pacific Ocean

PHILIPPINE
IS.

MARIANA IS.

Encounter
18 Aug 1944

GUAM

PALAU IS.

CAROLINE IS.

BORNEO

HALMAHERA

NEW
GUINEA

CELEBES

CERUM

To Perth

TIMOR

Arrived Perth
26 Sept 1944

AUSTRALIA

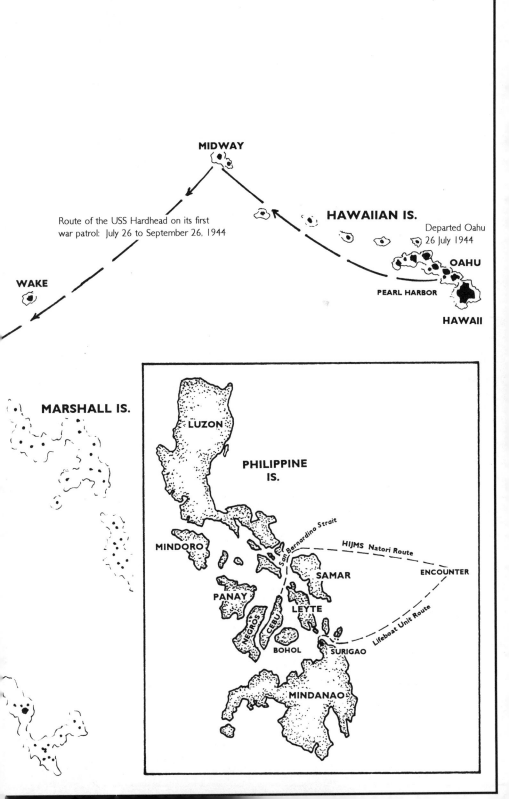

MIDWAY

HAWAIIAN IS.

Departed Oahu
26 July 1944

Route of the USS Hardhead on its first
war patrol: July 26 to September 26, 1944

OAHU

WAKE

PEARL HARBOR

HAWAII

MARSHALL IS.

LUZON

PHILIPPINE
IS.

San Bernardino Strait

MINDORO

HIJMS Natori Route

ENCOUNTER

SAMAR

PANAY

LEYTE

NEGROS

CEBU

BOHOL

SURIGAO

Lifeboat Unit Route

MINDANAO

9

August 18
Abandon Ship

Despite desperate pumping and jettisoning of heavy objects on the upper deck, nothing could prevent the ship from going down. About 0500, with the first gray of dawn, the forward deck was awash. The ship was still capable of steaming at six knots, stern foremost, a reflection of the heroic efforts of the engine room crew.

The captain caught sight of the chief engineer, who had come up on deck.

"I wish to speak with the chief engineer," said the captain, who then went down the bridge ladder. They were out of hearing range from the bridge and they seemed to be discussing whether efforts to save the *Natori* should be continued. The chief engineer shook his head frequently, a somber look on his face, as the captain appeared to be making doubly sure of the situation. But the chief engineer continued shaking his head.

When the captain reappeared on the bridge, he was wearing a snow-white class II uniform, carrying a sword in his white-gloved right hand. It was strictly forbidden to bring any object made of iron, such as a sword, onto the bridge, lest it disrupt the operation of the ship's gyrocompass. That the captain himself was violating this order indicated that he had definitely decided to give up further efforts to save the *Natori*.

Judging from the short period elapsed since he had finished

speaking with the chief engineer, it was evident that he had not gone to the captain's cabin at the stern to change into his class II whites. Instead, it was obvious that he kept a set of them in his sea cabin, below the bridge, to be prepared for a moment such as this.

As though confirming the captain's decision, the ship's speed gradually decreased until she came to a complete stop. Despite everything that had been done to save the ship, it was now merely a matter of time before the *Natori* would sink to the bottom of the sea. To save his crew, the captain passed the word man to man.

"All hands at leisure, begin making rafts, midupper deck."

The lumber the captain had loaded on board before we set off from Manila was now used for making rafts. About ten rafts were made by bundling the lumber and planks with ropes. Paymaster Ens. Takeshi Yokoi encouraged his men to distribute rice balls to the boats. Seeing this, the captain said, "Put some ship's biscuits and canteens on the boats." Then he passed the word: "Launch all boats. Jettison rafts into the sea."

Gunner's mate Ikeda was taking charge of the sailors nearby to launch the No. 1 boat. Other boats and launches were beginning to be launched one after another. The *Natori* took a list slightly to starboard, like a man with his head down a little to the right. The launching of the boats had to be completed before the ship's list increased, because the greater the list, the more difficult the launching would become. Behind the bridge near the torpedo tubes, heavy oil was seeping out of a crack, making the deck so slippery that the sailors launching the boats were having a hard time.

"Get the boats and launches away from the ship," said the captain. "Bear a hand." If they were not far enough away from the ship, the boats and launches would become entangled and go down with her when she sank. After confirming that they were well clear of the ship, the captain took a pack of cigarettes out of his pocket, and said, "Now, allow me my last luxury."

He lit two cigarettes at a time, and smoked them serenely in succession. His tone of voice and manner were not at all different from his usual way. I presumed he had decided that, because he had done all that was possible for him to do as captain, it was time for him to wait for the will of God. The captain passed the word: "All hands on deck."

At this order, the ship's company normally leaves their battle stations and assembles on deck. Because of the impact of the explosion, the jammed bulkhead door of the fireroom could not be opened, so the fireroom crew climbed up to the deck by cutting the wire nets of the ventilation ports. On the deck, buddies got together here and there, smoking cigarettes together. The *Natori's* huge hull gradually took a further list to starboard.

On the midupper deck, many crew members and passengers, about four hundred, were gathering. Captain Kubota walked out to the flag deck at the aft wing of the bridge, looked down at his crew and passengers gathered on the upper deck, and told them to give three cheers. He led them with, "Hurrah for HIJMS *Natori*," and then, "Long live the emperor!"

Directed by the medical corps officer, Surgeon Lieutenant Yoshimura, preparations were made to transfer the wounded and other patients to the launches.

On the bridge, the assistant navigator was encouraging his men to secure classified documents in places that could be locked, so that they would not be dispersed as the ship sank. The captain said calmly to him, as though a father were admonishing his son, "You won't be able to swim with a raincoat on, Mr. Hoshino. You should take it off."

Perhaps the captain was thinking of his first son, Lt. (jg) Isamu Kubota, about the same age as the assistant navigator, who was taking pilot training for a carrier–based dive bomber at Usa Naval Air Station (Ohita prefecture) in Kyushu. The previous May, while the ship was still in Japan, the *Natori's* officers had a party at a restaurant called Narumi in Beppu city. There the captain unexpectedly met his son, on shore leave and visiting the restaurant. A few days later, as the *Natori* was under way in Suo Strait, a dive bomber, rocking its wings, approached the *Natori* and circled over her as though it was bidding farewell. The captain was very much pleased with this, and believed his son had come to say good–bye to him.

Soon he returned to reality with a stern look on his face, and summoned the navigator.

"Mr. Kobayashi, the captain is now going to give you his views on the war and the lessons he has learned. These are his last words. The enemy is dominant and has taken the initiative in all the forward fronts. If we continue to let the enemy dominate us, we shall fight a war of attrition in vain. For the sake of our country, we must establish our final defense lines to correspond with our available strength and carry out operations independently and positively. By doing this we can fight against heavy odds in such a way that we will find a way out of the existing fatal situation."

"Captain, we want you to abandon ship with us now. Let's make a comeback someday soon."

This conversation was repeated several times. After a while, the captain dropped his voice and said, as though he were admonishing the navigator, "Mr. Kobayashi, take along as many young men as possible, and save their lives."

The navigator was so deeply moved by the captain's heart that he could not utter a word. Instead, he nodded his head deeply. The captain, in his white uniform, stepped forward to the wing, looking over his crew and passengers who had gathered on the midupper deck, raised his right hand high with his sword, and in a firm voice gave his last order as captain: "All hands, abandon ship."

The men on the midupper deck started to jump into the sea one after another. The captain, after confirming with his eyes that his men were abandoning ship, returned the salutes of those on the bridge, calmly walked down to his sea cabin, and locked himself in.

There was no time to lose, not even a second. Those at their battle stations on the bridge left on the double and jumped into the sea, then hurriedly swam away about fifty meters to avoid going down with the ship. Soon the *Natori* went down, as if standing on her head, waving her stern to the left. About twenty men, who probably could not swim, gathered on the fantail, lost their footholds, and tumbled down into the sea. The four screws, now stopped, made a pitiful sight.

After the No. 2 launch was set afloat on the sea, the crew pulled away from the ship's side. But she could make no headway against the wind and waves, and was pushed back to the ship's broadside. Ensign Ando and a few crew members were desperately trying to pull it away from the ship, but their efforts did not make much progress. Agonizing minutes passed. As the ship went down, one of the screws caught the No. 2 launch in a split second. The executive officer, the medical corps officer, Ensign Ando, and about fifty others aboard this launch were drowned in the whirlpool caused by the ship's sinking, and none of them were seen on the surface of the sea again.

The *Natori*, which had been in action continuously since the outbreak of the war and fought gallantly against the enemy, went down to the bottom of the sea off the east coast of the Philippines.

After submerging at 0600, we maintained our approach course to the target. Every five minutes or so the captain raised the periscope to survey the situation and get a range and bearing on the target. These data confirmed that it was dead in the water. At 0713, when the distance to the ship was less than 6,000 yards, we heard two explosions accompanied by rumbling noises. Six minutes had passed since the last periscope observation, and Captain McMaster immediately raised the periscope. I clearly recall how he said with amazement, "It's gone."

Over the next ten minutes we heard more than half a dozen distinct explosions, and a constant rumbling noise, like the noise made when two rocks are rubbed together under water. In retrospect, this was not unexpected, for the depth of the water in this area is about thirty thousand feet, one of the deepest spots in the Pacific Ocean; the increasing water pressure on the ship as it sank would cause various portions of the ship to collapse.

During this period the mood in the conning tower was subdued. On the one hand there was a sense of satisfaction, and even celebration, for our mission had been accomplished. This was heightened by our conviction that the target was a battleship, and the fact that, before this, no submarine had ever sunk a battleship.

There was also a feeling of amazement. We were a new crew in a new submarine. We had been in our patrol area less than a week, and already had this very significant success. Further, this had been accomplished without any countermeasures, and with relative ease in a bold surface attack at night.

There was also sadness in the air. We knew that many lives had been lost in the sinking of this ship. We firmly believed that ours was a just cause. The reality of war, however, and its impact for life or death on many persons came home to us with new meaning that day. This was not a time to gloat in our success.

At 0845 we came to radar depth and had two airplane contacts at a range of three to four miles and closing. Believing that these planes were searching for us, the captain decided that we would remain submerged and search the area for wreckage from periscope depth. This decision was welcomed by the crew, for we had been at battle stations since 0100, and most of the crew had little sleep before that, anticipating the arrival of the target in accordance with the top secret message we had received.

During the day a minimal amount of wreckage was sighted through the periscope.

Immediately after the *Natori* disappeared, I was gripped by a fear I could not ignore. The *Natori* was fitted with some ten anti-submarine depth charges on her fantail. The depth charges had a mechanism that, in response to water pressure at a preset depth, caused them to explode. This explosion would kill people swimming within a radius of a thousand meters. To set the depth charges to safe, the fuses had to be cut. Had anyone been prudent enough to do this in that utter chaos? A few uneasy minutes passed, which felt like hours. Thankfully, no explosions occurred. Later I learned that a special service torpedo officer, Ens. Masata Kato, had kept his head and had cut all the fuses.

Although I had been afraid of the possible explosion of the depth charges, I paid little attention to the rough sea. When my first worries were over, however, I suddenly began to feel uneasy about the stormy weather. Large swells were coming from the north, while the winds and waves were from the west. The water was covered with heavy oil, which began causing considerable irritation to my eyes. While I was concerned about the irritation, my attention was diverted from the waves, and in consequence I inadvertently swallowed heavy oil as well. I could not move my arms and legs freely with my uniform on and I found swimming was very difficult.

Some survivors, who probably had no prior experience of having their ships sunk, began to sing the military song "At Sea Be My Body Water-soaked":

At sea be my body water-soaked,
On land be it with grass overgrown.

The open sea was rough: big swells, strong winds, and high waves. It was more than enough for anyone just to swim, so their singing did not sound like a song and soon they quit. It was no time to indulge in the sentimental feelings about being parted from our beloved ship. I reminded myself this was just the beginning of our ordeal and that great suffering lay ahead of us. Then I swam to the nearby No. 2 boat and got aboard. The navigator, Lieutenant Kobayashi, also came aboard this boat after me.

After a brief period the navigator said to me, "Mr. Matsunaga, send this semaphore to the other boats: `Is the Executive Officer safe and sound?'"

"Aye aye, sir," I said, and semaphored as instructed, but we received no reply. Then he said, "Mr. Matsunaga, I believe that the executive officer has been killed in action. Send another semaphore saying that the navigator will assume command as the senior officer present (SOP) in the No. 2 boat." Then I sent the following semaphore: "Navigator Lieutenant Kobayashi is in No. 2 boat. Will assume command as SOP as of now."

Command was established in that way. Within our range of vision we could see two launches, three boats, numerous rafts, and many bobbing heads. There must have been about three hundred officers and men. Shortly after 0800, we heard a sudden outcry. It was from the No. 3 launch, which suddenly listed to starboard and went down. We found out later that the launch had been damaged on the ship's hull while being set afloat.

Chief Engineer Ishiguro and some fifty others had been aboard this launch, but the sea was so rough that the other boats could not possibly come to their rescue. We found some men swimming without jackets on, as though they had been swimming for pleasure. We warned them, "Hold on to a raft or plank, or you will be exhausted from swimming."

When things let up a little, I sat down on the bottom of the boat, and reflected on what had happened to us. The impact of the torpedo instantly plunged the inside of the ship into utter darkness. In that chaos, both the forward and aft magazines were immediately readied for flooding, preventing further damage to the ship by explosions of the magazines.

Special service gunnery officer Lieutenant Suzuki's pet phrase was, "Wherever I may be, in bed or in the head, I always make a practice of having a functioning flashlight dangling around my neck." Such preparedness for emergencies, which he had borne in mind at all times, enabled him to respond to the situation promptly and effectively in the complete darkness.

Special service communications officer Ens. Hichiro Yamaguchi had made studies on how to send out urgent dispatches when the ship was damaged. In preparation, he had stored amplifiers at separate locations, and carried out drills for setting up an antenna at night, in case the ship's antennas were brown off by an explosion. As a result, he and his men were able to string an antenna and send out urgent dispatches without delay. The fruit of his constant readiness was the ability to determine the length of the antenna corresponding to the wavelength to be used for transmission, and to know where to stretch it in the dark.

Yeoman First Class Ginji Yamamoto told me later about his

experience when he swam to the No. 2 boat: "When abandoning ship, my duty was to secure the roster of the ship's company. As I reached the boat, it was almost overflowing with survivors. Sir, not a soul, not a single one of those in the boat would dare lend me a hand. I was lucky, however, because a man from my department saw me and pulled me out of the water. Thanks to him, I survived."

The boat was in such a condition that it might have capsized if they picked up another survivor. That those in the boat would not lend a hand to strangers in the sea illustrates one side of the instinct of self-preservation. What a variety of emotions and responses an event like this brings out in human beings!

PART FOUR

ORDEAL IN THE STORM

10

August 18
The Boat Unit
Consisting of Three Boats

"Starboard ahead, port back!"

The boat officer was struggling against the rough seas as he tried to avoid capsizing the boat. It was a difficult situation, and he yelled out orders in a shrill voice. The men on the starboard side rowed to go forward, while the men on the port side rowed to go astern. When the boat finally responded to the boat officer's orders and began to swing its bow to the left in the rough waters, he yelled again.

"Starboard back, port ahead," to make the boat swing in the opposite direction. But the flustered men were confused, their faces distorted with pain and agony.

The sky had been overcast with thick gray clouds since morning, and the winds and waves were high. I had paid little attention to these conditions while I was on board our ship, but having abandoned ship and taken to the boats, things looked quite different. With strong westerly winds the boat would labor to the crest of a high wave, then suddenly drop into a trough, completely at the mercy of waves, like a leaflet.

To make the situation even more difficult, huge swells were coming at a slow tempo from the north. Thus the boat was forced to "dance" to a strange combination of tango and waltz. As the winds caught the boat and swept it sideways, it rolled dreadfully, and the boat officer had to order the bow of the boat first right and then left, so that neither waves nor swells would hit it broadside.

I was afraid that if this continued the men rowing the boat would become exhausted from this hard labor. Furthermore, I began to worry that after dark we would not be able to see the whitecaps, and it would be almost impossible to keep bringing the bow of the boat into them, which was essential to avoid capsizing the boat.

Then, it occurred to me that when I was a midshipman at the Naval Academy, I had seen an illustration of a sea anchor in one of the textbooks.

"Senior officer, I would like to make a sea anchor, sir," I requested.

"That sounds like a good idea. Go right ahead, Mr. Matsunaga," he replied.

I then addressed those in the boat. "Anyone who knows how to make a sea anchor, raise your hand." But no one did. Then I jumped into the rough sea, and pulled a plank aboard the boat. We then tied a sling (a piece of metallic gear used in raising a boat), which served as an anchor, to the plank, heaved it into the sea, and secured it to the bow of the boat.

The sea anchor kept the bow pointed into the wind with the waves and swells rolling past us. The boat officer then ordered the men to stow the oars, and take a rest, sitting on the bottom of the boat. They looked at one another as they gave sighs of relief. I then semaphored to the nearby boats and launch to make a sea anchor and drift. Soon after we had a reply from the launch.

"We are drifting downwind. Request towing."

We realized that the launch's fuel tank was empty, but it was out of the question for us to tow a heavy launch in the rough sea. Again, I semaphored to the launch to let out a sea anchor. They did not have the necessary gear to make one, however, and the launch drifted leeward rapidly, and was out of sight by midafternoon.

Originally, the *Natori* was fitted with three boats and three launches. When the captain received the Fleet Headquarters' advisory about off-loading the boats, he turned this advisory down and kept every boat and launch aboard. The other two boats continued to be within our range of vision, but one of the launches went down with the *Natori*, one sank shortly after it was launched, and the third was out of sight. There was little we could do but pray that the storm would soon be over.

The rafts that had been prepared on the ship gradually came apart because of the strong winds and big waves, and the provisions that had been loaded on them were lost. We observed that some men, after being thrown into the ocean by the violent up-and-down motion of the rafts, would crawl back on the raft, only to be thrown back into the sea again. As the rafts neared our boat, we encouraged the men by saying, "We will accommodate you in the boat when the sea becomes calm. Hold out until then."

We saw a man, all by himself, holding onto a piece of wood. I hollered to him, "Be careful not to get exhausted."

One factor in our favor was the water temperature. We were in the southern part of the Pacific Ocean, and the water was much warmer than we had expected.

It remained cloudy all day long, and when the sun set it suddenly grew very dark around us. The sea was still raging and had not subsided at all. For those of us who worked on the bridge, including the navigator, the assistant navigator, and myself, the communications officer, this was not an unusual experience, for the bridge was not lighted at night. Those who worked in places that were always lighted, however, felt very uneasy about the darkness in the boat.

During the night, when I had nothing to do for the moment, I lay down on the bottom of the boat, and absentmindedly began to reflect. I realized that I had already passed the low point of my emotions and was shifting to a more aggressive, purposeful attitude. In fact, I was keeping my composure more than I had during the last hours on the ship.

When a person's life is endangered he is startled and cannot think clearly and make cool, rational judgments. What comes to mind in such circumstances is not so much the theoretical knowledge he has learned, but the things he was repeatedly told in his childhood and the practical experiences that have helped him in the past.

As I reflected, the first thing I remembered was a story of "bottomless dippers" told to me by a childhood friend.

He said, "When the sea becomes rough in stormy weather, and some people drown in a shipwreck, they appear as ghosts in the next storm, scooping up seawater with bottomless dippers, and pouring it into a boat sailing in that storm. Before anyone realizes it, that boat has also gone down."

When I was told the story, I thought to myself that scooping seawater with bottomless dippers simply does not make sense. Now I was in the *Natori's* boat as a grown man of twenty-five years, who had served in the navy for the past eight years, and I found a new interpretation of the story. This fable reminds one that in stormy weather, because of tremendous external forces exerted on the ship's structure, rivets come out or nails work loose to the point where leakage can occur at most unexpected places. As I considered the story in this way, I decided from then on to pay close attention to the bilge water in stormy weather.

What I recalled next was an experience during my high school days when I climbed the mountains. During one summer vacation we climbed Mt. Seburi, which is about thirty-two hundred feet in height and about thirty miles from my hometown. Our leader was Mitsugu Ohkawa-san, who came from the high school I attended and was two years older. We set out on bicycles with mess tins and tents loaned out from the school. Until then, I believed that the only way to cook rice was to boil it in a pan on the kitchen stove. When he taught me how to cook rice in a mess tin, I was astounded, and I have never forgotten how tasty and rich in flavor that rice was.

After dinner one evening the young leader asked me how to determine directions in a strange place. I replied, "By using a compass."

"A compass may become faulty or may be lost," he responded. "If you depend only on a compass, you will be at a loss under such circumstances. You should rely on more practical know-how. To find directions on a mountain, walk around a large tree. If you see moss growing on the trunk of the tree, that side is north. In a city, look at school buildings. They are built in an east-west direction, so that the sun will shine in each classroom as the sun moves across the southern sky."

I was astounded at his remarks. Ohkawa-san was only two years older than me, but he had far more insight and practical knowledge. I decided that the key difference was his experience in mountaineering. Soon afterward I followed his lead and joined the mountaineering club of our school.

Mr. Masaichi Okamura, a teacher in our school who led the club, was not a hard man to get along with during his classes in Japanese language and Chinese classics, but when it came to club activities, he was a strict disciplinarian. If you had failed to bring even a single item you should have brought along, he would not let you go to the mountain with him, even if that item did not seem to be important for that day's mountaineering. He believed that if a person had a casual mental attitude toward mountaineering, he would likely end up in an accident someday, and therefore was not entitled to be a member of the group. Furthermore, if you defaced the mountain, he would exclude you from subsequent activities. He said the mountain was the creator, that is, the deity itself, and anyone who would deface the deity was not entitled to climb the mountain.

When I was a few years older, Mr. Okamura led a party of ten students on a climb of Mt. Kuju, in Ohita prefecture. When we reached the peak we were captivated with the breathtaking, magnificent view. Suddenly thick white clouds appeared all around us, accompanied by terrible thunder and lightning, and visibility was reduced to less than two meters. We panicked and began to run down the mountain.

Seeing this, the teacher shouted, "Halt! Listen to me. Do as the leader tells you to, or you will endanger your lives."

He instructed us to remove everything made of metal from our clothes, and lie face down on the slope of the mountain, separated from one another. The teacher predicted that the storm would soon be over, and he was right. It was his firm and sound instruction that prevented a possible disaster. By this experience, I learned how easy it is for a group of people to panic, and how important it is to stop a panic before it begins.

Another memory came to mind concerning an incident when I was a midshipman second class at the Naval Academy. One weekend, when I was a crew member of a boat that set out for a cruise in the Inland Sea, the boat ran aground at Ohnasami Jima (next to Miya Jima near Hiroshima), and was damaged.

When the boat ran aground, everyone was confused and uncertain as to what should be done, but Midshipman Ariyuki Nagoya, who was in charge of the boat, drew himself up to full height and called out, "Okay, you guys, have cool heads! Don't let a single thing drift from the boat. This is the off-load priority: first, fittings of the boat. Next, things loaned out for the cruise from the academy. Last, your blankets. Now, get going!"

Midshipman Nagoya was afraid that disciplinary action would be taken against him at the academy, but when he reported to the OOD and told him the details of the accident, the OOD said, "It is regrettable that the boat was damaged, but the emergency measures taken after the accident were very well done. No fittings of the boat were lost, and the accident report was filed by telephone promptly. In an emergency, few people can make sound judgments and act with full presence of mind. The command and leadership exerted by Midshipman Nagoya has left nothing to be desired. Well done, indeed."

Thus, in my midshipman's days, I learned by experience how

important a leader's judgment, decisions, and subsequent actions are in an emergency.

As I looked up from my reflections, Seamen Second Class Ono and Yasui were sitting in front of me, looking very innocent, but also confused, and uneasy. Who could blame them? Although they were in the service, they were only lads of seventeen, about the age I was when I was scared to death and exposed myself to danger at the top of Mt. Kuju.

Up to now I had been helped, either directly or indirectly, by a great many people. Now I was the second in command of the *Natori* boat unit. To repay my indebtedness to those who had helped me in the past, I recommitted myself to being the best possible leader for my subordinates in these difficult circumstances.

11

August 18–19
Ordeal

"What time is it now?" someone asked. On the ship we casually asked this question many times, but it had a strange sound when asked in a boat drifting in the Pacific Ocean in complete darkness. I replied, "2300 hours."

"Mr. Matsunaga, you must have a luminous watch. Thank you, sir."

It was so dark that I could not recognize who spoke, but I felt he said this in gratitude. Looking at my luminous watch I thought of Capt. Tamotsu Takama, the captain of the battleship HIJMS *Haruna*, and of the occasion when I bought this watch.

In April 1941, immediately after I received my commission, I reported aboard the *Haruna*. Because I wanted to make a favorable impression on the captain, I saluted him especially politely after being logged aboard. He responded, "Ensign Matsunaga, a naval officer doesn't have to be good at saluting. Instead, I want you to be a smart officer when your superiors are not around, and especially in a crisis. To achieve this, you must train diligently in your specialty at all times. Is that clear?"

"Aye aye, sir. I shall do my best to train diligently in my specialty at all times." I was deeply impressed by the captain's words, because he saw through my superficial motive and got to the heart of the matter.

A little later, the *Haruna* made a port of call at Yokkaichi harbor in Mie prefecture, and the crew was permitted to visit Nagoya. It was in Sakae–machi, the busy shopping quarters of the city, that I bought this luminous watch as a souvenir to begin my career as a naval officer. Now it had been soaked in the seawater, and because it was not completely waterproof, it would soon stop ticking. Until then, it would remind me of Captain Takama's counsel, "A naval officer must be competent and work effectively in a crisis."

At 1530 we surfaced in a rainsquall and began a search of the area, but found nothing of significance. Early that evening we transmitted a message by radio to our base reporting on developments of the past twenty–four hours.

At 2040 we entered an oil slick that appeared to cover several square miles. Ten minutes later the radar operator detected a plane at a range of four miles and closing, so we dove immediately. We had also picked up a signal that indicated the plane was equipped with radar.

At 2110 we came to radar depth, and after determining that all was clear, we surfaced. We were still in the oil slick and tried to get a sample of the oil. However, the oil film was too thin, and we abandoned this effort. At 2200 the captain set our course westward toward San Bernadino Strait at fifteen knots.

Suddenly, in the complete darkness of night, we heard the sound of engines, and a tense atmosphere, entirely different from that of fighting high winds and waves, filled the boat. Every man was staring at the face of the senior officer, watching him with bated breath.

This sound was not that of an airplane engine, but the diesel engines of a submarine. As the boats were made of wood, their radar could not pick us up, and since we were not lighted, their lookouts could not see us either. The two men at the bow immediately began to get the machine gun ready to open fire, but I knew that a machine gun would not be effective against a submarine. Furthermore, if the gunners should fire it by mistake, we would immediately be detected. I shouted to the gunners, "The enemy is a submarine. The machine gun won't do any good. Don't fire until I say so."

I listened carefully to the sound of the engines. Was it just my hopeful imagination, or was the sound gradually diminishing? Yes, the sound was fading, and before long utter stillness prevailed again.

On the ship, we had determined directions by a compass, and wind direction and velocity by a wind indicator. But now we had to use our best judgment to estimate such factors merely from observations. In this way we concluded that the submarine had surfaced to leeward not far from us, and then proceeded leeward away from us. By using radar they would surely know that the *Natori* had gone down to the bottom of the sea. Nevertheless, we wondered why she surfaced. Was it to charge the batteries, or to take prisoners? I was encouraged by the fact that if we proceeded westward into the winds in the morning, we would be getting farther away from the submarine.

Shortly after midnight, the winds and waves increased, and soon afterward a severe rainsquall poured on us like wet pebbles for twenty minutes or so, then was suddenly gone. We breathed a sigh of relief, but the soaking wet clothing stuck to our bodies, making us feel sick and miserable, and we began to shiver with the terrible cold wind, which had a velocity of twenty-five knots or more. The men in the boat huddled together to keep warm, and waited, longing for the dawn. It was a long, long night–the longest night we had ever known.

The conditions were awful for the men in the boats, but they were even worse for those on the rafts. As the sea was raging, they had to keep a good distance between rafts to avoid hitting one another, but being separated like this made them feel lonely in the darkness. "Ahoy," they would call to one another. As the night advanced, their calls became fewer and fewer, and everyone was longing for daybreak.

The men who had been on the rafts told us later about their experiences and thoughts during a long, difficult night: "The winds were so strong that we felt very cold. When we couldn't stand it any longer, we jumped into the sea to keep warm. But if we stayed in the water too long, we got tired and climbed back on the raft again. We repeated this until daybreak."

Out of necessity we had all learned how to face Nature's ordeal.

12

August 19
Dawn after the Long Night

Finally daybreak appeared and the long night was over. It was August 19, the day after the disaster. The sun, which we had eagerly awaited for warmth and encouragement, did not appear all day. It not only rained all morning, but the strong westerly winds continued throughout the day. The whitecaps all around us looked as though they were white devils' teeth, scoffing at the men in the boat, who were soaked with the rain and shivering with cold.

I passed the word for everyone to have breakfast when they chose, but no one bothered to eat anything. The wet clothing coiled around our bodies making us very uncomfortable and miserable. We were thoroughly chilled by the wind and had completely lost our appetites. I decided that I should have a drink of water to keep up my strength. But when I pulled out the tap of the breaker, I found not even a drop of water was left in it. On the ship, the breaker had been filled with water, but every bit was now gone. I felt conditions were getting worse and worse.

Time was passing slowly, and our hearts and minds were depressed, when about 1000, we heard the sound of airplane engines above the low-hanging clouds. Was it a friend or foe? We were uneasy and everyone was looking up, holding his breath. Then we spotted it for a moment, as it flew through an opening in the clouds. We were overjoyed, for it was a friendly medium–attack bomber. With a ceiling of only fifteen hundred feet, the plane had to fly at very low altitudes, which restricted the forward visibility from the cockpit. We wondered if they spotted us under such adverse conditions, and began to feel doubtful.

As our doubt was about to turn to impatience, the bomber returned, rocking its wings. It had spotted us! We had no way to communicate with the plane, however, which was very frustrating. The "rising sun" markings on its wings were clearly visible and reassured us. We were truly grateful to the crew of this bomber for having spotted us in such adverse weather conditions. To express our thanks, some shouted out, while others took off their jackets and waved them to the plane as hard as they could. The plane flew over us in a wide circle twice, and then, on a third run, dropped a message cylinder.

The message read: "Two friendly destroyers on their way for rescue. Please feel at ease. 761st Air Group, Flight Petty Officer First Class Yamada."

A rubber raft was also dropped near the message cylinder, with a package of rice balls attached. It was obvious that the crew had sent us their own lunch. Their deed expressed, much stronger than words, the commitment of men at the front who were willing to share all they had with others. With the message that rescue ships were under way, some men in the boat danced for joy, as though they had sighted the ships.

Sometime after the bomber flew out of sight, we saw a man swimming toward the boat. It was almost thirty hours since the *Natori* had gone down, and it seemed impossible that he had been swimming all along. However, without his life jacket on, he was stroking neatly. He must have been extremely self-confident, for he seemed to have every intention of continuing to swim.

We repeatedly urged him to get into the boat, but he declined our offers. According to a colleague who had joined the navy with him, he had had a hard time of it in a boat when his previous ship had been sunk. Sadly, he was not among those who made it ashore.

In the history of naval disasters, those who took off their clothes intending to swim ashore almost invariably did not survive, whether their ships sank ten miles or a few hundred miles from shore. Conversely, many of those not proficient in swimming, who drifted until rescued or swam ashore holding on to some floating object, survived.

During that day we kept a sharp lookout for the No. 1 launch, which had drifted to leeward, but did not sight it. Because of the storm, it was impossible to search for it. We decided to wait until the storm subsided, and then to look for it by forming a line abreast with our three boats.

A raft neared our boat, with Ensign Hoshino, the assistant navigator, and five others on it. Ensign Hoshino's eyes had been so badly damaged by the heavy oil floating on the surface of the sea that he could not open them, and having coped with the raging sea while blinded, he was exhausted. At this time there were about thirty men in our boat, which had a design capacity of forty-five, so there was ample room in the boat to accommodate everyone from the raft.

Bringing these men on board, however, posed a delicate problem for the senior officer. He was Ensign Hoshino's immediate superior, and accommodating him could easily appear as favoritism. Sensing the senior officer's thoughts, I decided to tactfully intervene, and suggested that Ensign Hoshino be moved to the boat. Even so, I recognized that if we set a precedent and began accommodating all the men on rafts as they came to the boat, it would be filled to capacity in no time. Further, I was afraid that accommodating only those groups among whom was an officer could lead to criticism afterward. Finally, as an alterative to accommodating all six men, I shouted out, "Mr. Hoshino is in bad shape. Someone trade places with him."

Not a single soul stood up and responded to my words, and under these extreme circumstances, I could not possibly designate one person to give up his place in the boat.

Finally Ensign Iwa, the assistant recognition officer, asked to trade places with Ensign Hoshino, although he had been in the officers' sick bay suffering from diarrhea for about a week, and had returned to duty only four days ago. Although Ensign Iwa had not yet completely recovered from his illness, and had swallowed some heavy oil while in the water before reaching our boat, he had assumed the duties of boat officer in the No. 2 boat. Now he offered to change places with his senior, Ensign Hoshino. But Ensign Hoshino would not accept his subordinate's heroic proposal.

Finally, the navigator, who was the immediate superior to both officers, intervened and had them exchange places. To reward Ensign Iwa's admirable spirit, the navigator gave the men the rubber raft and the package of rice balls the bomber had dropped, and moored the raft to the stern of our boat.

The storm became even more intense late that night. The boat responded differently to the wind and waves than the rubber raft, so that the painter mooring the rubber raft would slacken one moment and suddenly stretch taut the next. If we allowed this to continue, the rubber raft would have capsized, or else the painter would have parted. After some discussion, we decided to cast off the painter, promising the men in the rubber raft that we would take them into the boat on the following day. No one had the slightest idea of the consequences of this decision.

As far as provisions were concerned, scores of rice ball lunches and two big tin cans containing ship's biscuits were in each boat. When I was a lad, a neighborhood friend, Masato Matsueda, told me that many mutinies on ships had been caused by matters related to food and drink, not with allowances for food, whether enough or not, but with unfair distribution.

So, beginning the day after the disaster, food was strictly rationed, and everyone was given exactly the same amount of food, regardless of his position, rank, or rating. As the second in command, I enforced this rule. To convince the men in the boat that the food was strictly guarded against theft, I threw myself over the two large cans of biscuits whenever I slept.

At this point we also worried that the enemy submarine of the previous day might return and were grateful that the day passed without its appearance.

PART FIVE

STRATEGY AND DECISION

13

August 19
Challenge to the Navy's
Common Knowledge

That afternoon, as the men in the boats were beside themselves with joy because the rescue ships were headed for us, the
senior officer called me to the stern.

As I casually looked at the bow, I noticed that almost all the
men were carefully observing the senior officer and me. This
reminded me of an instructor's words at the Naval Academy: "In
an emergency, every subordinate will look at the face of his commander."

We turned our backs to the men, looking to the sea, and
talked so that they would not hear what we said or see the expressions on our faces. He asked, "Mr. Matsunaga, what is your opinion
about the situation?"

"Under the circumstances, I would conclude that we should
not stay in this area and wait for the rescue ships, sir."

With this introductory remark, I told him the following story.

"On October 11, 1942, during a sea battle off Savo Island, I was
aboard the heavy cruiser *Furutaka* when it was severely damaged by
enemy bombardment and could not maneuver. We then requested
our Fleet Headquarters to dispatch rescue ships, and were informed
that four destroyers had already been dispatched. But the *Hatsuyuki*
was the only one to come to our rescue, even though only two
hours before, the *Furutaka* had been operating with all four destroy-

ers. That only one of the four could locate us testifies to how difficult it is to find a ship at sea in the darkness of night.

"After I was rescued by the *Hatsuyuki*, I went up to the bridge where the navigator, Masahiro Rai, a classmate of mine, told me, `You know something, Matsunaga? The *Furutaka* had drifted far to the west from her reported position. That is why we barely made it before the *Furutaka* went down.'

"In our situation, the destroyers mentioned in the medium-attack bomber's message are steaming to Palau with supplies, and more than likely they will give priority to their original transport mission. If so, it would take four or five more days before they or the No. 3 Armed Transport would arrive in these waters on their return trip. Further, we have no flare signals to indicate our position to the rescue ships, so even if they did arrive in the area, there is only a slim chance they will locate us. Therefore, my conclusion is that we should not remain in these waters."

After listening to my explanation, the senior officer agreed. "I don't think we should stay in these waters either. Make a plan to proceed to the Philippines right away, Mr. Matsunaga."

I was quite startled at his words. Although I didn't think we should remain in this area, this did not imply that we should make our way to the Philippines. I could not utter a word in response, but I must have looked as though I thought it was absolutely impossible. The senior officer reproved me with a harsh tone.

"Look, Matsunaga, the men here are not like a herd of cattle. They are survivors of the *Natori*, which means they are selected members of the Japanese Navy. Everything we have, from the structure of our boats to each oar, is based on the traditions of our navy, so a great many of our seniors are watching over us. Why do you think you cannot make a plan?"

"Aye aye, sir. I will make a plan to proceed to the Philippines. Please allow me some time for preparation."

As I began to conceive of a plan to make our way to the Philippines by boat, I remembered the boat races we had at the Naval Academy. One involved rowing a distance of two thousand meters in less than twenty minutes, while another race was twelve miles in about two hours. In either case, the races took place in late fall or during winter, when it was cool, so that the crews would not become exhausted from the heat. But, in our situation, we were three hundred miles from the Philippines, a distance about twenty-five times that of the longer boat race, the season was summer, and the place was the southern Pacific Ocean. Also, we would have to keep rowing for at least ten days, with limited food and water, and we had no navigation equipment or charts.

The many negative factors for a successful voyage to the Philippines could readily be cited, and the only positive factors were the few that had been mentioned by the senior officer during our conversation. Therefore, considering all the factors, the plan seemed doomed to failure.

As I was considering how to navigate three hundred miles in the Pacific Ocean without using any navigation equipment or relying on any landmarks, I reflected on people that had navigated the oceans in history, particularly the Phoenicians, the Vikings, and the Polynesians, who were well known for their ocean navigation.

The Phoenicians were the first to circumnavigate the continent of Africa, probably by 600 B.C. However, they were never far from land, and therefore could readily stop for supplies, anchor near shore in stormy weather, and use coastal, rather than celestial, navigation. So I decided there was not much to be learned by recalling the accomplishments of the Phoenicians.

The Vikings rowed down the west coast of the North Sea from the eighth to eleventh centuries and invaded the coasts of Great Britain and Scotland. Some courageous Vikings sailed into the North Atlantic Ocean, and discovered Iceland and Greenland, and established colonies there. Later some went down the east coast of the North American continent, and reached what is now New England. I thought the Vikings must have had some form of celestial navigation, though most of their activities were limited to the familiar North Sea.

The accomplishments of the Polynesians is an amazing story of superb seamanship and navigation, for during the Stone Age they achieved a mass migration over some four thousand miles in small vessels and with only primitive navigation equipment. My conclusion was that, if at all possible, we should follow the Polynesians' art of navigation.

A key element in their approach to navigation in the Northern Hemisphere, as in our situation, was their ability to use Polaris (the North Star) in their navigation. When one is at the equator, Polaris is due north on the horizon, and as one travels north from the equator, the altitude of Polaris increases. Thus, Polaris not only indicates north, but its altitude indicates the latitude, or how far north of the equator, you are. Apparently the Polynesians developed some devices to measure the altitude of Polaris.

The Polynesians also knew much about the direction and

velocity of prevailing winds and currents, and how to set a course to take advantage of them. This knowledge, along with their skills in navigation, enabled them to make the round-trip from Tahiti to Hawaii.

No one knows just how the Polynesians learned their skills in seamanship and navigation, but it is clear that once learned, the elders passed the knowledge on to the next generation. In a sense, this was also our experience at the Naval Academy, where we learned astronomy and the fundamentals of navigation from our instructors.

It is not clear whether the Polynesians knew in advance their destination when they migrated, but we know that it was a small, remote island probably difficult to find.

To our advantage, our destination, the Philippine Islands, was well known to us, stretching some twelve hundred miles north to south, and only three hundred miles away. Mt. Mayon, the volcano on Luzon Island, over nine thousand feet in height, would be a prominent landmark. It had a small crater at the top and a skirt spreading out at the bottom, and from certain directions it resembled Mt. Fuji.

Also, because it was the monsoon season in this region, we could expect frequent rainsqualls, which meant we were blessed with a heaven-sent gift of water. In addition, we were all the *Natori's* survivors, and we had considerable harmony among us.

As I considered our many advantages–favorable winds and current, frequent rainsqualls, and a spirit of cooperation and harmony–I was beginning to think we had a chance of success. To make doubly sure, I decided to consider our drawbacks compared with those of the Polynesians and, if possible, to devise ways to counteract them.

One disadvantage was food. The Polynesians took with them preservable foods for the voyage, such as dried screw pine nuts, sweet potatoes, baked breadfruit, dried fish, and live chickens.

In contrast, all we had were some ship's biscuits, and there was no way to overcome the lack of food. I recalled again my youthful friend's advice about mutinies at sea, and I renewed my resolve to deal out the rations equally.

Finally, I considered faith. For the Polynesians to successfully make these migrations, the leaders had to have a firm faith that the voyage would be successful, and also that everyone in the group felt confident of success, dissolving fears. This was where myth was important to the Polynesians.

According to their myth, their god Tane made the first woman out of the earth. She was given life by his charm and her firstborn child was a Polynesian, which meant that the descendants of the Polynesian had directly inherited the flesh and blood of their god. As a result, the Polynesians believed that they were blessed with divine characteristics, a belief of utmost importance to them as they made their way to unknown places, for it encouraged their faith and erased their fears.

This religious perspective extended to the construction of their ocean vessels. Shipwrights had high social status, ranking second only to the priesthood. When building their vessels, they fasted, purified their bodies, and placed their building materials and lines under their god Tane's protective care. Launching ceremonies were solemn occasions; all the inhabitants participated in the celebration and blessing of the ships.

Because these convictions were a part of their lives, there was no chance of a mutiny, and each succeeding generation challenged unknown waters as they exercised faith in their god and their vessels, avoided taboos, and developed confidence in themselves.

What did we have in comparison?

During the early years of the Japanese Navy, probably there were some faiths or taboos. But in 1937, when I enrolled in the Naval Academy, there were few taboos, though some faith still existed.

Midshipmen of the Naval Academy visited Kotohira Jinsha, a shrine in Kagawa prefecture, at least once while at the academy. Before the war, it was a time-honored practice for crews of warships, steaming off the coast of this shrine, to collect money from crew members, place it in a wooden barrel with a flag showing the ship's name attached to it, and drop it into the sea. The fishermen living near the shrine who picked up the barrel would dedicate it to the shrine on behalf of the crew.

When I visited the shrine, the owner of one of the souvenir shops told me a story of how miraculous this shrine was:

"Once upon a time, a vessel encountered stormy weather and drifted far from shore. The skipper lost sight of land and didn't know which way to turn. Then he prayed with his whole heart to the shrine, and set a stick upright. He then proceeded in the direction in which the stick fell, and soon he found himself within sight of land."

This story may well have been true, but I had received professional training in the art of navigation, and was not quite ready to believe this story, and so did not buy a charm. Even if I had the charm of Kotohira Jinsha with me now, I thought, I could not convince the men of the boat unit that this is how we should determine our course.

Now, as I was trying to formulate a plan to proceed to the Philippines, as the senior officer ordered, I realized that by the conventional thinking of the navy, this was impossible. But, comparing our situation with that of the Polynesians, I realized that our major drawbacks were the lack of food and of faith. However, we were far better off in the composition and experience of our crew members, the quality of our vessels, our knowledge of navigation, having a positive destination and a known route to travel, and the prospect of frequent rain. I was beginning to think that there was a chance that our plan would succeed, but only if we could avoid a mutiny on our way.

14

August 19
Brainstorming

Two other officers were aboard our boat besides the senior officer and me. They were the ninth division officer, Lt. Shuichi Yamashita, and the assistant navigator, Ens. Akio Hoshino.

I believed that it was essential that all hands consent to the plan to proceed to the Philippines by rowing, and as a first step I decided to talk to these two officers about it. To avoid a dispute or a hasty conclusion that this couldn't possibly be successful, I broke the ice as follows:

"I think officers must be able to make sound judgments under any circumstances. So, let's do an exercise together. Given our present situation, if we wait and the rescue ships arrive, we will be saved. But suppose things develop so that we no longer expect rescue ships, and we would start rowing toward the Philippines. In that case, what contribution could you make?"

The assistant navigator replied right off the bat.

"Mr. Matsunaga. I will prepare a navigation plan. We are now about three hundred miles east of Samar Island in the Philippines. This area is in the northeasterly trade winds region, and the North Pacific Current also flows at half a knot westward. So, it is very favorable to go west from here. If we row in pairs, we could make a good three knots. By rowing ten hours a day, we could cover thirty miles, which means we would reach shore in ten days by my calculation. Taking into account stormy weather or other unfavorable circumstances that might slow down the progress, I would say that fifteen days will be required for the voyage. The Philippines stretch out for twelve hundred miles from north to south, so if we keep rowing to the west, we will surely hit one of the islands."

"Mr. Hoshino. Your remarks to keep going to the west sounds very simple. Proceeding to the west by sighting Polaris abeam to our right looks simple enough theoretically. But don't you think it would be more difficult than you expect?"

"Sir, Orion is near the celestial equator and Scorpio a little to the south. At this time of the year these stars, as viewed from any point on the earth, rise in the east and set in the west. Therefore, while they are in the eastern sky, we proceed by turning our backs to them. Conversely, while they are in the western sky, we proceed toward them. Thus we would be moving westward. By doing so, we could solve the problem you have just mentioned."

"Mr. Hoshino, I will go along with your plan. But suppose we proceed to the west according to your plan, and five or ten days later we find ourselves in the wrong place. Then it would be too late to redo the voyage. Are there some ways to check our positions en route? By the way, Mr. Yamashita, how could you contribute to this outfit?"

"I can make a sail for sailing, and I will observe fish and birds to estimate the distance to land. If we proceed according to Mr. Hoshino's plan, we will have to row ten hours a day for fifteen days, which means we must expect to go through all sorts of hardships. I will try to give the men a dream, a dream to look forward to."

The assistant navigator sank in thought with his head a little to one side for a while, and then responded. "Mr. Matsunaga, I have an idea. To check our position on our way, we could use changes in the latitude and longitude. First, let me tell you how to determine the latitude. Stretch your right arm fully out, and then place your thumb horizontally over the horizon with your index finger slightly upward. The tip of your index finger will then point at fifteen degrees of altitude. We are now at twelve degrees north, so the altitude of Polaris is also twelve degrees. The first knuckle of your index finger should point at twelve degrees of altitude. From the relationship between Polaris and your index finger, we will be able to know the change in latitude.

"I will also explain how we can measure the change in longitude to determine the distance traveled. We will time the sunrise each day by watch, and compare the difference in time between the sunrise of today and that of yesterday. Strictly speaking, there is a small time difference in the sunrise of each day. But I think that if we regard the sun as rising at the same time every day, the error will be negligible for all practical purposes. Knowing the circumference of the earth at this latitude we can calculate the distance we traveled from the difference in the time between sunrise of each day."

"Mr. Assistant Navigator, to be honest with you, I've never thought about using Orion and Scorpio to guide us westward, much less confirming our positions by measuring the latitude and longitude as you indicated. As far as navigation goes, you are a genius, indeed!"

"It goes without saying that I can check our positions on our way as well as navigate our boats, as long as I have a watch, sir."

Seaman Second Class Ono, who had not studied astronomy or the theory of navigation, probably did not fully understand the conversation between his superior officers. But seeing close at hand how confident the assistant navigator was, and how he apparently convinced the communications officer, his senior in rank, reassured him. The words "as long as I have a watch" must have given a sense of relief to Ono and the other men in the boat.

Then I told the two officers, "Up to now, I have encountered all sorts of disasters at sea as well as on land, and know what it's like to be close to a panic. I think I know the psychology of people in distress. I should be able to contribute psychological guidance to the men."

It would be an exaggeration to say that our conversation had been carried out in a holiday atmosphere, but it was done during a slack period as we waited for the arrival of the rescue ships. Because it was not a crisis situation, everyone spoke freely, and we exchanged views freely and without hesitation. In those days we did not have the concept we now call brainstorming, but that in essence is what we were doing.

As August 19 dawned, the *Hardhead* was heading west on the surface toward San Bernadino Strait, and had cleared the area where the encounter with the enemy ship had taken place. At 0530, we made a trim dive to ensure that the boat was prepared for any emergency dives that would be necessary that day. This was a good decision, for throughout the day many aircraft were visually sighted or detected by radar, and we had to dive on each occasion. A summary of the ship's log for that day provides some details:

0808	Radar contact with aircraft, 7 miles. Dove.
1010	Surfaced
1057	Sighted one Oscar–type plane, 4 miles. Dove.
1135	Surfaced
1251	Sighted one unknown–type scout bomber, 6 to 8 miles. Dove.
1400	Surfaced
1500	Detected enemy radar. No contact on our radar.
1504	Sighted one Hap or Zeke, 3 miles. Dove.
1954	Surfaced
2012	Sighted one unknown type plane, 2 to 3 miles. Dove.
2128	Surfaced. Changed course to 090. Too many planes around here to suit us.
2257	Sighted low wing single engine plane, 2 to 3 miles. Dove. This plane was sighted by two lookouts. We were beginning to think that the lookouts were "seeing things" until now, but began to think about radar–equipped torpedo planes instead.
0038	Surfaced
0307	Headed south for our own area off Surigao Strait. Feel sorry for the boat that gets this area if it is like this all the time.

With this thought we put the encounter with the enemy ships behind us, and shifted our focus to effectively patrolling the area to which we had been assigned.

15

August 19
Fatigue Sails in the Sunset

The ninth division officer, Lieutenant Yamashita, asked the men to offer odds and ends of their fatigues, and sewed a sail with a needle made of a piece of wire. Then he set up a spare oar as a mast, and used a large and a small boat hook as improvised yardarms. He did all this with the ease of an extremely practiced hand.

The senior officer exclaimed, "Hey, Number Nine, you're a dyed-in-the-wool seaman!"

The assistant navigator joined in with his praise.

"Mr. Yamashita is a seaman rather than a naval officer. You are so skilled with your hands!"

"The objective of the training we received at the Naval Academy was to make us proficient as seamen as well as good naval officers," I said. "When we were diligent and quick in our practical duties, our instructors commended us for being good midshipmen. But if I remember correctly, we were rarely praised for being skilled in tying knots or good at boat handling, as competent seamen are. Number Nine, in making his comment, the senior officer gives you his highest praise."

Lieutenant Yamashita replied humbly. "I was born in a town near the coast and was brought up with the sea as a playground. I think I am a little more used to the sea and ships than those brought up on land."

We semaphored to other boats to have them make sails. The No. 3 boat quickly hoisted a smart sail. As we learned later, Master-at-Arms Watanabe of the operations department, who was used to sewing sails, was in that boat. In addition, Leading Seaman Saito had two fatigue jackets on, and offered one. Lieutenant Tsuchiya became the officer in charge of sailing, and Petty Officer Watanabe was his assistant in the No. 3 boat.

The tropical depression still remained in the area that day; westerly winds were blowing at wind force five, which is fifteen to twenty knots. Taking advantage of the wind, the ninth division officer lost no time in showing his skill at sailing. The boat, its bow tilted a little leeward, moved forward in silence as though it were gliding on the surface of the water.

A big shout of joy arose in our boat. The seamen who had no experience in sailing rejoiced with wide open eyes. They were talking cheerfully and shaking hands with each other. The ninth division officer had given our men a dream to hold on to, as he had promised. Thanks to his efforts, the gloomy mood that had prevailed in the boat lessened.

As we were sailing with an oar as an improvised mast, and a sail made of sewn pieces of fatigue jackets, the speed was slow compared with a regular sailboat. Further, with only one sail, we could not tack into the winds, which meant that an inexperienced sailor could easily handle the sheet. I was developing a great trust in Mr. Yamashita's broad-minded understanding and his ability to contribute to our efforts.

"Say, I recall when a long-range boat race had to be held twice." With this introduction, I told the following story to Mr. Yamashita and Mr. Hoshino. "In the fall of 1939, when the annual long-range boat race from Eta Jima to Miya Jima was held at the Naval Academy, the ninth department was victorious in the race. But then it came out that the winning crew had off-loaded a sling and two spare oars to reduce the weight of their boat. Then Vice Adm. Koki Abe, the vice superintendent of the academy, passed the word that the race must be repeated. After the second race was over, he admonished the midshipmen with the following speech:

"'It goes without saying that a person should strive to win a race at all costs and with all his might. But at the same time, the race must definitely be fair for all. One should never compromise sound judgment for the sake of winning the race. Always consider the possibility of a sudden accident and be prepared for emergencies. A sling can be substituted for an anchor, and a spare oar for a mast or a rudder. To emphasize this to all hands, I order that the race be rerun.'"

Mr. Yamashita's sailing was now being done exactly how we were advised by the vice superintendent.

The stormy weather continued throughout that night. We were still dragging a sea anchor, and therefore didn't have to worry about being capsized. Because there was nothing to be done at the moment, I reminisced about when I was attached to the training squadron, and received my baptism of a storm.

In August 1940, 288 brand-new ensigns out of the Naval Academy (68th class) were aboard the training ships *Katori* and *Kashima*, together with eighty engineer ensigns (49th class of the Naval Engineering Academy) and thirty paymaster ensigns (29th class of the Naval Paymaster Academy).

We were about to set out for a long cruise from Shanghai to Southeast Asian countries, when it was suddenly called off by the authorities in Tokyo. We then immediately shoved off for Yokosuka Naval Base. Unfortunately, it was the typhoon season, and we were accompanied by a typhoon all the way home from Shanghai. The climax of the storm occurred during the last leg of our trip.

I was asleep in a hammock at night, when the beam just above my head began to creak and groan. Then the layer of paint on the beam peeled off and fell on my face. This shocked me, for I considered the ship a floating castle in which I placed much trust.

On the following morning we passed a wooden vessel that was rolling and pitching in the waves like a leaflet. Lt. Comdr. Masanobu Kawamata, the engineering staff officer of the squadron, explained what was happening.

He said the length of an iron ship and the length of the waves are not necessarily the same. As a result an iron ship can be subjected to great stresses during a storm. However, because a wooden vessel is shorter and has much less draft, it experiences less stress, and in a storm is much stouter and better off than an iron ship. This is especially true for a small wooden vessel.

Our boat never creaked and groaned during the storm, which assured me that the boat was quite reliable, and I murmured, "Lieutenant Commander Kawamata, it's been four years since you taught me about the stresses on different kinds of ships during a storm, and thanks to you I realize that this small boat is quite safe and reliable in a storm. But young sailors are discouraged in thislittle boat. Now I think it is my turn to be a good leader for them."

16

August 19
Tyrannous and Cruel Sea

A flash of lightning was soon followed by a clap of thunder. This was not surprising, for thunderstorms are frequent and often severe in the Philippine waters. Because no other objects were over the open water, and we had several metal pieces on board, such as the machine gun, we were deeply concerned that we might be struck by lightning. The boat was already filled with many people, so there was no place to hide.

Seamen Second Class Ono and Yasui were beside me, wondering aloud, as they looked at each other's face, if the lightning would strike our boat. Then I asked, "Ono, do you know an old saying, 'There is no need to fear thunderclaps in the direction of *tatsu mi*. They are only a roar'?"

"No, sir, I don't know," he replied.

"Okay, then, I will tell you what it means. Yasui, you listen to me too."

With this introduction, I told them the following tale. "In my childhood, when my grandmother found me scared from the sound of thunderclaps, she taught me this old saying. At that time I thought she was speaking gibberish. But after I learned meteorology at the Naval Academy, I realized the truth of this statement.

"First, let me explain what `tatsu mi` means. In our country, the points of the compass have symbols of `juni shi`, or the twelve signs of the ancient oriental zodiac, and `tatsu mi' corresponds to south-east. So, the old saying could be interpreted as `thunderclaps in the southeast only roar.'

"In Japan, and where we are now, the weather moves from west to east, so those thunderclaps heard in the southeast will move farther eastward, and are nothing to fear."

The sea was still raging. After more than five years of sea duty, I thought I was well aware of the power and variability of the sea. Now I realized that looking at the sea from a huge ship was one thing, but experiencing it in a small boat was quite another. On the ship we were protected from the wind, rain, cold, and heat, but here in the boat, nothing was between us and the winds and rain, much less cold and heat. I had to confess that in these past few days, as we drifted in our boat in the vast ocean, I learned for the first time the true nature of the sea. The sea lacks restraint and control. It is like a parade of huge emotional ups and downs. It resembles the tyrant Nero, violent and cruel. But this tyrant does not go for any flattery or deception. Instead, sea duty requires an ability to live by wit and determination, and animal–like reflexes. A moment of slackness or one mistaken rudder order can ruin a whole ship's company.

When I told the senior officer that I wanted to talk to him about the storm, he again took me to the stern of the boat.

"Senior officer, I assume this tropical depression is moving to the north, where it may develop into a typhoon as it nears Japan. I have heard that the semicircle on the east side of a typhoon is a danger area. Therefore, I suggest we proceed to the west, which will take us farther from the storm."

The senior officer responded, "If we had a wind direction indi-cator, anemometer, and barometer, we would know the intensity of this storm. We don't have such gear, so all we can do is estimate the position of this low from the wind direction, and move away from it as much as possible.

"There is a tradition among seamen about a typhoon. `In the northern hemisphere, with the wind at your back, stretch out your left arm, and in the southern hemisphere stretch out your right arm. Your outstretched arm will point to the center of the storm.' Through this tradition, you can estimate the direction of the center of a typhoon, and steer the ship to move away from it.

"Old–timers learned meteorology as time–honored wisdom rather than theory. As you said, the east side of the typhoon is a danger area, and by proceeding to the west, we can get away from the danger area.

"Because a tropical depression increases in intensity as it moves northward, the low we have encountered here is in its infancy. We have suffered from the storm for the past two days, and I don't think it will develop any stronger than it is now. Anyway, the sea anchor is very effective. In my opinion, I think it is much safer to drag a sea anchor and sit tight rather than move westward in the storm.

"Incidentally, Mr. Matsunaga, what in your opinion is the capacity of our boat?"

"By the regulations, the capacity of a nine-meter boat is forty-five men, sir. But this figure was derived considering heavily clothed men and a raging sea in the cold north. Here in the south, where we wear light clothing and the sea is calm, I would say we could accommodate fifty men, or even more, without impairing the safety of the boat, sir."

"As near as I can determine, the capacity of the naval boat was established in the regulations after considering various conditions, such as rowing, sailing, or towing, under which the boat was navigated. As commanding officer of this outfit, I want to save as many men as I possibly can. I think we could accommodate more than sixty men easily, so long as in a storm, we don't proceed, but drag the sea anchor, and wait for the storm to pass. What do you think, Mr. Matsunaga?"

"I agree. If there's a storm we will drag the sea anchor and wait for it to pass. I don't think we should stick to what the regulations say. Let's check physically to see how many men we can accommodate by measuring the freeboard of the boat. We shouldn't forget that the reason we could make a sea anchor was that the captain passed the word to tie down the lumber on the upper deck with manila ropes. If wires had been used instead of ropes, they would surely have gone down to the bottom with the ship, sir."

"I reported to the Fleet Headquarters in Manila with the captain when we were making arrangements on the mission," the senior officer continued. "Their staff officers strongly recommended that we off-load the boats to increase loading capacity of the ship, but the captain refused because the boats were necessary to save the ship's company in an emergency. Instead, he ordered to off-load the spare torpedoes and made arrangements to load the lumber for use by the passengers aboard the ship.

"Just before we abandoned ship, he instructed us to bring the ship's biscuits and water canteens with us. Because of his insight we can now manage our meager living.

"Remember when the baby named Yoichi was born on the ship some time ago? The captain rejoiced over this event, saying that Yoichi was his rebirth. I paid little attention to his word `rebirth' then. I realize now that he was calmly prepared for the last moment. Despite this, he gave much consideration to how to save the lives of his subordinates. I sincerely have to take my hat off to him. As the *Natori* came to a stop and was going down, he entrusted me, on the bridge, with delivering his views on the war to the Fleet Headquarters in Manila. I must make this report at all costs. If I do not, I will not know how to apologize to the captain's soul."

Petty Officer Masaji Kawai had suffered serious burns in the fire caused by the explosion. When he managed to swim to our boat, he was in an extremely feeble condition. Without medical supplies, all we could do was lay him down on the bottom of the boat. He frequently asked for water, but we had none. He breathed his last at 1400. After sunset, we buried him at sea, quietly and sorrowfully, with all hands offering a silent prayer for the repose of his soul.

17

August 20
We Shall Succeed, on My Word

The second morning dawned. As I looked around the horizon, not a thing was to be seen, including the other boats and rafts that were supposedly not too far away from us. If they had capsized during the night, there should have been some wreckage, but I did not see anything at all on the water. Again I realized how terrible the storm had been the night before.

During the night I slept awkwardly on the bottom grating, and now all my joints ached. Even so, I could feel that the rolling and pitching of the boat had lessened considerably. The other men, lying on the bottom of the boat, had also sensed that the raging sea had begun to calm down and started expressing their hopes.

"It's got to clear up today."

"I can hardly wait to see a bright daybreak."

"The sun will surely bring us some wonderful gifts."

I did not want to pour cold water on their enthusiasm, but I was remembering that scorching day, six months ago, when our ship, the light cruiser *Naka*, sank at Truk Island, and how I learned very decisively that the sun is not always a friend.

We were glad to see the sun after the storm and looked forward to this new day, but our joy was short-lived. Only an hour after sunrise the direct rays of the sun and reflected heat from the sea began to scorch us mercilessly. We felt like chickens roasting in an oven, and our exposed hands and feet pricked as though stung with needles.

As the sea calmed down, we decided to search for the men drifting on the rafts and to accommodate them in the boat. The wind had been westerly on the previous evening and was still blowing toward the sun, so we figured that the rafts, which had no sea anchors, would have drifted farther to leeward than our boat, and began searching in that direction. To be spotted easily by other boats and rafts, we set up a spare oar as a mast and hoisted an ensign atop of it, a good object to be seen in a distance. We had rowed for some time when the lookout reported excitedly, "A mast, right twenty degrees, distance unknown!"

Some men overreacted, and began to make a fuss that a res-cue ship was coming to save us, but it turned out to be the No. 1 boat. A little later, we sighted the No. 3 boat approaching from far to leeward. Although no arrangements had been made, we found that each boat had set a spare oar as a mast, and hoisted an ensign at its top. That each boat independently took steps to improve their visibility indicated that all hands were becoming accustomed to their sea duties, and I began placing much confidence in these men.

The three boats assembled close together for the first time since the disaster. When we had abandon–ship drills on the *Natori*, each person was assigned to a specific boat or launch, but we found that this had not been carefully followed. The first, second, and sixth division officers and the paymaster were aboard the No. 1 boat, but only a few officers were in the No. 3 boat. Therefore, the senior offi-cer passed the word to the second division officer, Lt. (jg) Yasuhisa Kubo, to transfer to the No. 3 boat as boat officer. He also decided that Mr. Yamashita should remain in the No. 2 boat, so that he could glean from his knowledge and experience as he made deci-sions. One might say that he was appointing the headquarters staff of the boat unit.

Our next concern was locating the men who were still on the rafts. To do this, the senior officer deployed the three boats in a search formation: No. 2 boat at the center, No. 1 boat on the left, and No. 3 boat on the right. We then began a search to leeward, and soon sighted many rafts. They had been damaged by the storm, and most of the provisions had been carried away by the sea. Each boat began picking up the men on the rafts and any who were in the water. The No. 3 boat semaphored us, "Have accommodated the maximum capacity of forty-five men. Request your instructions for further actions."

The senior officer replied, "Disregard prescribed maximum capacity of the boat. Accommodate every man within range of vision. Notify immediately upon sighting of No. 1 launch or rubber raft."

When everyone on a raft or in the water had been picked up, more than sixty men were in each boat. Sadly, we never found the No. 1 launch and the rubber raft. The thought of leaving them was heavy on us, but at 1400 the boat unit made a 180° turn to head for the Philippines.

If we had complied with navy regulations, we could have accommodated only 135 men in these three boats. Instead, we had 195 men in the three boats, fifty percent more than the prescribed capacity. The senior officer's affection for his subordinates was important in his thinking, but the decision was based on his conviction that this could be done safely, given the quality of our boats, and the water conditions in which we would navigate.

Soon after heading westward, we discovered many cardboard boxes floating in the water. As we approached them, I thought "That's it!" They were boxes containing canned peaches and tangerines, which we desperately needed to quench our thirst and supplement our food supply. But on picking them up, we found that the contents of the boxes were gone, and they were merely empty boxes. The bottoms had come open during the storm, and with disappointment we left them behind.

At 1600, the senior officer assembled the three boats and passed the word: "Action orders. The *Natori* boat unit shall depart here at 1900 on this day and proceed to the east coast of the Philippines by rowing and sailing. The estimated time for the voyage is fifteen days. Make the provisions on hand last for thirty days. We shall succeed, on my word."

Objections of "It's impossible, sir!" and "It's reckless!" arose among the men because of a conviction that rescue vessels were on their way.

Chief Petty Officer Watanabe stood up to speak. "I beg your pardon, Senior Officer, but I would like to say a few words. I'm a son of a fisherman on the Japan Sea. A tradition among fishermen is that when you have a disaster at sea, do not move about at random, but sit tight. We are very well aware that our boat unit belongs to the navy, and we are naval personnel. But, we now have neither arms nor propulsion engines. In other words, we are in the same situation as fishermen. So, I respectfully suggest that we follow the fishermen's wisdom and stay here until the arrival of the rescue ships."

"I am fully aware of this tradition among fishermen to remain at the scene of a disaster," replied the senior officer. "But you must also remember this tradition was developed in peacetime. The war is on now, and the situation is entirely different. Saipan and Tinian in the Mariana Islands have already fallen into the hands of the U.S forces, and it won't be long before the enemy lands in the Palaus and the Philippines. We cannot expect rescue ships to come, and even if they did, looking for boats in the vast ocean is like looking for a needle in a haystack. If we had flares to draw the attention of the rescue ships, there might be a chance, but without them, the possibility of being sighted by rescue ships is very small.

"There is another important point. Whether you like it or not, the friendly reconnaissance plane observed that there were three boats and many survivors at the scene of the *Natori's* disaster. As you know, the navy assumes that a boat will never sink. Therefore, if we do not get to shore, the *Natori's* entire crew, six hundred men, would not be considered killed, but missing in action. Then those who did die in action would simply be listed as missing, and we would do a great disservice to Captain Kubota and four hundred others who went down with the *Natori*.

"Furthermore, we could not face our families who say prayers to God and Buddha day and night for either our triumphal return or meeting glorious death in action. So, we must reach shore at any cost."

The senior officer did not assert his authority, but persuaded the crew through reason and admonition. No one spoke a word, and a dead silence fell over the boats.

After a while, Petty Officer Watanabe stood up again and said, "Senior Officer, my heart is at peace that even if I die as a beggar at sea, it will not matter much as long as I am recognized as killed in action. But if I will be regarded as missing in action, it is an entirely different story. This is more than I can bear. Therefore, I will fight to the death and strive at any cost to live. Please take us to the Philippines, sir."

Voices of "You're darn right" and "Come on, let's go" arose. The crew agreed that we would voluntarily and willingly fight our way through by rowing. And, in the end, it was a collective decision to proceed to the Philippines. It is a well-known fact that groups are stronger when decisions are made collectively rather than having orders formulated and passed down by higher authorities. I was very much pleased we reached a consensus.

However, I knew that this was not a group decision originally, because it had been made by the senior officer, and the men merely concurred. I was afraid that there might be some among the crew who believed all decisions should be made by majority rule, and would not accept the chain of command on many important matters. When a group must work together for a long time and under difficult living conditions, there must be no question who is to make decisions and issue orders. For our crew, the senior officer had the rightful authority to determine such important matters as whether to go on or to turn to the right or left. I decided I would have to make this point at a more convenient moment.

The plan for this voyage was presented to all hands. During the day, each boat would set up a spare oar as a mast, and hoist an ensign atop it so that we could easily be spotted by friendly aircraft or vessels. Also, each boat would sail in a westerly direction, but would remain within sight of the other boats. The leading boat would be at the center of the formation, with one of the other boats on each side. During this time, crew members would take turns to lie down for some rest, and prepare for the rowing at night.

At night, the No. 2 boat would take the lead, with the No. 1 and No. 3 boats moored in order behind. We would row in pairs and there would be four shifts of rowers. Each night we would row for ten hours and determine our direction by observing the stars.

The senior officer decided that before rowing began each night, the boat officers would assemble for a thirty-minute briefing. When the three boats gathered together, he would issue the orders and explain his judgment of the situation not only to the officers but to all hands.

Before our departure on this long voyage, we had each boat report the provisions aboard, and redistributed them evenly. Each boat received two large cans of ship's biscuits, some compressed rations, high-calorie aviation rations, and a few cans of condensed milk. If sixty-five men on each boat consumed it as usual, the food would have lasted only five days, but according to the plan, we would make the provisions last for one month, and continue rowing for fifteen days. This meant that the ration for each person was two meals a day, each meal consisting of one three-gram biscuit. The size of the ration was the same for every crew member regardless of his status, rank, or rating.

PART
SIX

EN ROUTE TO THE
PHILLIPPINES

18

August 20
Under Way

Before departing, the senior officer directed that a final search be made for the No. 1 launch and the rubber raft. He passed the word for each boat to deploy in a different direction, yet remaining within sight of one another. After searching for some time, the other boats semaphored that they had sighted nothing. Then the senior officer ordered the boats to assemble again, and we offered a sincere prayer for the souls of Captain Kubota and the four hundred others who had cast their lot with the *Natori*.

The *Natori* boat unit was organized as follows:

Life Boat Assignment	*Natori* Assignment	Rank	Name
Commanding Officer	Navigator	Lt.	Eiichi Kobayashi
Leading Boat Officer	Communications Officer	Lt.	Ichiro Matsunaga
2d Boat Officer	Torpedo Officer	Lt.	Choji Murano
3d Boat Officer	2d Division Officer	Lt. (jg)	Yasuhisa Kubo

When the time came to depart, we made the planned formation for night navigation, the leading boat at the head and the other boats moored in order behind. The senior officer passed the word: "Now we shall start rowing to the Philippines. Place the oars in position. Ready, give way!"

Each boat began to pull oars simultaneously. Most of the men had never rowed in pairs before and they hit one another and often caught a crab. Their performance was so poor that the boats did not pick up much speed. According to the assistant navigator's plan, we were to make three knots, but our speed was only one and a half knots–half as much as planned. In the western sky, about to turn into darkness, the new moon was throwing its dim light over the waters, and noctilucae, which we had not expected to observe in the waters so far from shore, dimly illuminated the stern of the boat.

Soon after departing, I noticed the senior officer burying his face in his arms, and not stirring an inch. We had picked up all the men on the rafts and in the water, and had accommodated 195 men–135 was the prescribed maximum capacity. Still we had not been able to find the No. 1 launch and the rubber raft despite all our efforts.

The senior officer must have felt distressed about the crew of the rubber raft, for he had promised, when they released the painter the night before, that they would be accommodated in the boat when the storm was over. He undoubtedly would have continued the search had there been a reasonable prospect of finding them, but the ocean was so vast that we could not expect to find the launch or the rubber raft, even if we stayed in the area a couple days longer. To delay might also have prevented him from carrying out the captain's orders to deliver his last words to the Fleet Headquarters in Manila.

Perhaps burying his face in his arms indicated that in his heart he could not stand the implications of his decisions. I wanted to speak some comforting words to him, but it would not have helped, for I had no solution to the situation. I felt heartless and cold-blooded, but I could do nothing but pretend that I had not seen his behavior. The men in the boat were rowing so diligently that hardly any of them saw that the senior officer was downcast.

The three officers in our boat were discussing the senior officer's confidence and determination about this voyage to the Philippines. The assistant navigator brought out a point.

"I wonder why the senior officer did not mention 'trusting in divine favor and aid' in his orders?"

After some reflection, I responded. "In the Japanese Navy,

when we are about to carry out a difficult mission, it has been traditional to say `trusting in divine favor and aid.' These words imply that we pray for divine aid on the way. I think the senior officer wanted to show his mettle and determination that we would make our way to the Philippines under our own power, and decided not to mention these words on purpose."

The ninth division officer said, "This voyage by boat is surely death defying. Yet he did not mention a word about writing a final letter to loved ones. What do you think of it, Mr. Matsunaga?"

"Such a letter is written on the assumption that one is going to die. The senior officer is determined to deliver the captain's views on the war to the Fleet Headquarters in Manila, and he is not thinking of himself or his men dying. We are not going to die, so why do we need to write that kind of letter? I'm sure this is why he purposely avoided mentioning this matter."

The senior officer was convinced that this voyage would not succeed if each boat proceeded on its own. Because we did not have a chronometer or a compass, we had to determine the heading by observing the stars. Four officers could read the stars: the senior officer, the communications officer, the ninth division officer, and the assistant navigator, all of whom were aboard the leading boat. This assured that the men in the other boats would not know the direction to go unless they followed the leading boat.

That evening the sky was lighted brilliantly with the splendor of the setting sun, the first dazzling sunset we saw in the boat. The new moon and the Southern Cross were side by side, just above the southwestern horizon. Within a few hours, both would disappear below the horizon.

Looking at the northern sky, I sighted Polaris first. In Japan, the altitude of this star is about forty degrees, high in the sky; the Big Dipper and Cassiopeia play supporting roles. Here in the Philippine waters, where the latitude is twelve degrees, Polaris is just above the horizon at an altitude of twelve degrees.

Viewing the sky as the face of a clock with Polaris at its center, the Big Dipper was at ten o'clock and Cassiopeia was still out of sight below the horizon. The sky rotates from east to west, counterclockwise on the axis connecting the celestial North and South poles. It would be another three hours before Cassiopeia appeared in the northeastern sky to take the place of the Big Dipper as the clue to finding Polaris.

Scorpio was twinkling in the southeastern sky at an altitude of sixty degrees, posing as though it were a monarch of the nightly sky. As we would be sailing on a westward course without a compass or chronometer, we would have to depend on Antares, the brightest star of the constellation of Scorpio, for the time being. I thought, Hi, Antares, you look awfully red tonight. Don't tell me you are drunk. Be a dependable guide for us, won't you?

At 0300, Scorpio disappeared below the horizon in the west as though its role were over. Finally Orion, which would appear as our guide in place of Scorpio, appeared sometime after 0330. This constellation lies near the celestial equator, and always rises in the east and sets in the west, and therefore was a dependable guide for us.

Rigel was twinkling blue and Betelgeuse red. They looked like a large airplane with three stars on its fuselage and red and green navigation lights on its wings. Extending the line that connects the three stars on the fuselage of the imagined airplane to the southeast, you find Sirius. When we were aboard the training squadron as newly commissioned ensigns, we took a fix on stars by sextant every morning and evening. In the morning, as the stars disappeared one after another as morning dawned, Sirius was the last star that remained in sight. For beginners, Sirius, the brightest of all the stars, was the easiest to measure its angular distance from the horizon with a sextant.

Because the senior officer was determined to reach the Philippines, it occurred to me that I, the second in command, should do all I could to get the officers and the enlisted men to cooperate with his decisions. My first step was to tell the ninth division officer and the assistant navigator of a terrible experience I had aboard the light cruiser *Naka*.

"On a bright, sunny day in February 1944, the *Naka* was attacked at Truk Island by enemy carrier–based aircraft, and the forward fifty meters of the ship was torn off and sunk. The men whose battle stations were on this part of the ship had to abandon ship by jumping into the water. Between the third and fourth attacking waves, boats were lowered to rescue the survivors. Fortunately, I was picked up and taken to the aft part of the *Naka*. While I was in the water, my eyes were contaminated with the thick film of heavy oil floating on it and began to hurt.

"All the engines of the *Naka* had been damaged and were now stopped. We decided to use the only means of communication available and semaphore to a nearby submarine chaser for assistance. Because no signalman was aboard the aft part of the ship, I climbed up the mizzenmast, and semaphored to the submarine chaser, ignoring the throbbing pain in my eyes.

"Soon the fourth attacking wave began and the aft part of the ship also went down to the bottom. Fortunately, most of the ship's company in this part of the ship were rescued by the submarine chaser.

"That night my eyes were so swollen that I could hardly open them. The medical corps officer of the ship reprimanded me: `Mr. Matsunaga, when you were picked up the first time, you should have had your eyes washed to clean out the heavy oil. Why didn't you do that? It was entirely out of the question for you to work under the scorching sun without having your eyes treated. If you leave them as they are, you will surely lose your eyesight. What you must do is cool them off with a wet towel all night.'

"My classmate, Takuzo Taji, cooled my eyes with a wet towel all night long, without sleep or rest, and thanks to his kind efforts, I did not become blind."

Then I stressed to my fellow officers that based on my experience, the fact that it was cloudy for the previous two days meant that we, the survivors of the *Natori*, were certainly blessed with God's protection.

After midnight we had a severe rainsquall. We were grateful to heaven, for one cannot live without water. But, if I may be allowed to say so, I wish it had been in the daytime, when the sun was shining brightly on us. A rainsquall by day would not only quench our thirst but cool us off as well. Rain at night might prevent a dry throat, but afterward it froze us.

19

August 21
Sailing at the Mercy
of the Wind

On the following morning, August 21, I found the senior officer plumped down on the stern sheets, looking over the crew with an air of composure. He had completely put aside the sentimental feelings of the previous night, and now assumed the solemn attitude of a commanding officer.

Our fatigues, which had become soaking wet with the rain-squall during the night, coiled around our bodies and made us feel miserable, as we eagerly awaited the sunrise. Soon the sun was shining brightly, as it had the previous day, and before long the heat became unbearable.

The ninth division officer said, "Mr. Matsunaga, it's so darn hot here that I can't stand it. Let's arrange the oars so that we can hang our jackets over them to make a shelter." The assistant navigator added, "How about taking turns and pouring seawater over the shelter? I'm sure we will feel a lot cooler due to the evaporation of the water, sir."

"I don't think it's a good idea, Mr. Hoshino," I responded. "We are sweating a lot even though we don't do any work. If we pour seawater over us now, we'll be sure to get inflammation of our skin."

The ninth division officer disagreed. "Mr. Matsunaga, the rain-squalls we encounter almost every day will wash the salt off our bodies. Therefore, we don't need to worry about skin inflammation."

His argument changed my mind. "Yes, you may be right, Mr. Yamashita. Let's set up a shelter now. I guess two heads really are better than one, as the saying goes."

After obtaining the senior officer's permission, we wasted no time in setting up an improvised shelter. Lying on our backs in the shade of the shelter, I began shooting the breeze with the ninth division officer. "Hey, Number Nine (we usually called him 'Number Nine', instead of ninth division officer), remember that yesterday we ran before the winds all day, but today the winds have died down completely! Why?"

"Among seamen, there have been sayings like these, Mr. Matsunaga: 'With favorable winds four hundred miles can be covered in one day, with no winds only two miles in twenty days.' 'A storm is a paradise for seamen, while a lull is hell.' And, 'A ship is at the mercy of sails, and sailing at the mercy of the wind.'

"Each implies that you cannot sail as you wish. Yesterday the winds were favorable, and you want the same winds to blow today. I think that is a bit too much to ask, Mr. Matsunaga. As you know, the sea has many merits you don't find on land. If you make the currents and winds work for you, you can go a long way effortlessly."

"You know, Number Nine, to change the subject, when I was a kid, I read quite a few books on great swordsmen. I remember reading that while a samurai was asleep on a futon [a thin mattresslike quilt placed on the floor for use as a bed], he was suddenly awakened by quiet footsteps of a burglar walking on a porch, and grabbed his sword close to his bedside to confront the intruder. When I read that I thought it was impossible, but for a long time after I was rescued when the *Furutaka* sank in the Solomon waters, I found that I was awakened by the smallest noise, even when I was in bed on land. Then I realized that I was acting with animal instincts after my life had been endangered. I guess that in old days, when doors didn't have locks, samurais made an effort to keep their animal instincts, even when asleep.

"Now, on this voyage to the Philippines, we have intellectual issues, such as finding the correct heading in this vast ocean, but we also need animal instincts to predict meteorological or hydrological changes. Let's leave the intellectual side to the senior officer and assistant navigator, while you and I stick with the animal instincts. Okay?"

"Mr. Matsunaga, someone told me a story of a downed pilot,

HIJMS *Natori*

USS *Hardhead*

Capt. Satoru Kubota, captain of the HIJMS *Natori*

Lt. Eiichi Kobayashi, navigator of the HIJMS *Natori* and senior officer of the *Natori* lifeboat unit.

HIJMS *Natori*. Seletar Dockyard, Singapore, April 1943

Comdr. Fitzhugh McMaster, captain of
the USS *Hardhead*.

USS *Hardhead* during shakedown on Lake Michigan, April 1944

Japanese lifeboat, rowing in pairs

Japanese lifeboat with design capacity of 45 persons on board

Japanese lifeboat with 65 persons on board, the situation in each boat
of the *Natori* lifeboat unit.

Equipment in a Japanese lifeboat unit

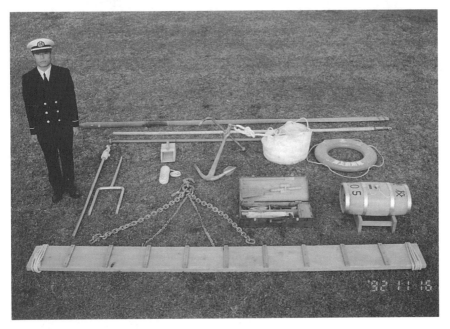

General MacArthur, President Roosevelt, Admiral Nimitz, and Admiral Leahy on board tha USS *Baltimore* at Pearl Harbor on July 26, 1944, the day the *Hardhead* left on her first war patrol. (Naval Photo Service)

Mr. Ichiro Matsunaga, Capt. Fitzhugh McMaster, and Mr. Kan Sugahara, November 1988

Mr. Ichiro Matsunaga and Capt. Fitzhugh McMaster at The Army and Navy Club, Washington, D.C., November 1988. (Courtesy The Army and Navy Club of Washington, D.C.)

Dr. Gordon J. Van Wylen

Mr. Kan Sugahara

Mr. Ichiro Matsunaga

who had made an emergency landing in a jungle in Borneo. As he walked in the direction toward his home base, he came to the bank of a river. He wanted to cross it but he found that many alligators were in the river, and he did not know what to do. Suddenly an idea struck him. He remembered the Tarzan movies he had seen many years before. He selected an ivy vine that was coiled around a tree on the bank, and cut it near the root. He then crossed the river by applying the principle of a pendulum. To survive in a combat area, whether at sea or on land, I guess you cannot do without the animal instinct. What I want to do next is give the men a dream to look forward to."

After a moment he said jokingly, "I should have eaten all three mangoes as you did, Mr. Matsunaga. But now it is too late. However, there is no difference between us, for we both have had the experience of having our ship sunk."

About 1400 the assistant navigator spoke to me as he stretched out his right arm and pointed.

"Mr. Matsunaga, this direction is south, sir."

"Hey, Hoshino, that must be a wild guess. How can you tell the direction without a compass, sir?"

"It's not a wild guess, Mr. Matsunaga. With a watch we can determine the direction of due south in this way. Hold your watch so that the short hand points to the sun. Then the bisector of the angle formed by the line connecting the center of the watch and the numeral twelve and the short hand indicates south, sir."

"Mr. Hoshino, you are indeed the brains of the *Natori* outfit. Don't hesitate to say whatever crosses your mind."

As nothing was to be done during that day, I reflected upon what is involved in rowing a boat. On land you might direct the movement of a group by having men line up in the order of their height and give commands such as, "Right, face!" or "Forward, march!"

When it comes to rowing, one cannot simply give commands. Our destination was the Philippines, and there were many important details of each person's assignment, such as one's position in the boat when rowing, when to take one's turn, and knowing how to row. Sixty-five men were aboard; four were officers and the remaining sixty-one were enlisted men. We decided to exclude the senior officer from the duty roster, and treated him as the commanding officer of the ship. The rest of the officers took one-hour shifts as the duty officer of the boat unit, or the boat officer of our boat.

Of the sixty-one enlisted men, thirteen had been seriously

injured or exhausted and were not in physical condition to row. We divided the remaining forty-eight into four groups. There were twelve thwarts, numbered one through twelve. The odd numbers, numbering from the bow, were on the starboard side, and the even numbers were on the port side. The thwart pitches for the first two rows were relatively narrower, the last two a little wider, and the middle two the widest.

Therefore, short men were assigned to thwarts one through four, medium-built men to thwarts nine through twelve, and well-built men to thwarts five through eight. In the navy, those assigned to thwarts five through eight were the driving force of the boat and were considered honorable roles. The men assigned to positions eleven and twelve were pacemakers, and had to be manned by men with a strong sense of responsibility.

When we were ready to begin, each oarsman sat down at his respective thwart. When the command, "Place oars in position" was given, each oarsman would place his oar in the oarlock, put his feet on the thwart ahead of his, and posture himself for the required back and forth motion of the upper half of his body. At the command, "Ready, give way!" he would bend his body forward and at the same time thrust out his arms all the way forward. Then he would push the water forcefully aft with the blade of the oar as he tilted his body all the way backward, pulling the oar close to his breast with both arms. As he lifted the oar out of the water he would rotate the oar around its longitudinal axis, and repeat the entire motion.

There are two methods of rowing; single, one person on each oar; and in pairs, two persons on each oar. In pairs, the two oarsmen sit side by side on the same thwart. The inner oarsman must only pull the oar backward; the outer oarsman performs the rotation and forward motion. Because we had to go three hundred miles to the Philippines, we decided to row in pairs, in four shifts, taking turns every hour, one hour on the inner thwart, another hour on the outer thwart, and then two hours' rest.

Because sixty-five men were in a boat whose normal capacity was forty-five, those off duty were forced to keep low in the boat, out of the way of the oarsmen. If one popped his head up by chance, he would surely be hit with an oar moving back and forth. So, even when resting, the men had to pay close attention.

This was the first time that most of the men had rowed in pairs, so they didn't have the knack of it, and their bodies hit one another, and they often banged their fingers and scratched their hands. According to the plan, we were to proceed thirty miles a day. After rowing for ten hours that night, everyone was completely exhausted. But despite our hard work, the boats had covered only half this distance. Some among the crew were ready to give up the plan as hopeless. If this happened we would never make the voyage to the Philippines, so I proposed to the senior officer that we should extend the working hours to meet our goal of thirty miles per day, but he turned down my proposal.

That day, at the boat officers' assembly, the senior officer gave the men a pep talk.

"Theoretically, rowing in pairs should be easier, because two share the task normally done by one man. But in reality, it does not work out this way," he said. "I recall that at the Naval Academy, each year of our upper-class years we would row in pairs for the long boat race from Eta Jima to Miya Jima. Although we thought we were used to it, at the beginning of the race we found we were very clumsy rowing in pairs. Most of you have never rowed in pairs before, so it is no wonder that things didn't go smoothly. With time, you will get the knack of it, and the boats will advance quickly. So, you don't have a thing to worry about. Keep at it."

The senior officer gave this talk to the crews to keep them from getting discouraged, and as the second day rolled into the third, they rowed harmoniously. At first, I observed that they were merely keeping strokes with one another, and did not really bend to the oars, which concerned me because we could never reach shore at this pace. However, the men were conscientious naval personnel who had considerable sea duty, and from the fourth day on they pulled good oars. By the fifth and sixth days, the boats were advancing more and more vigorously.

During this period I reminisced about the boat training we had taken at the Naval Academy. Midshipmen must serve as seamen as well as naval officers, and we were trained for both. The practical training to develop our abilities was done using the boat. In one exercise, we were divided into groups of about fifteen, and each group tried to deliberately capsize the boat. We found that the boat had such dynamic stability that it was absolutely impossible for us to turn it upside down in the water. Next, the boat was deliberately submerged by unscrewing its drain plug, and we found that the boat still never went down. Through this hands-on training we realized that these boats are unsinkable and gained great confidence in them. Through this teaching and experience, we acquired the grounding to become competent commanding officers who could cope with unexpected situations and emergencies at sea.

Now the senior officer, who had undergone such training at the Naval Academy, could make crucial, death–defying decisions under extremely difficult circumstances. He knew we had only one chance to reach the Philippines, and we could not redo things if we made mistakes. Sometimes he had to make decisions opposed by most of the men in the boat.

We who served as boat officers had also gone through the same hard training in rowing, single at times, and in pairs at others, until completely exhausted. Therefore, we knew very well from our experience how fatigued one can become from rowing, and this influenced our behavior toward those who did the rowing.

Not until our second year at the Naval Academy did we learn to row effectively singly, and only then did we begin to row in pairs. But now Seamen Second Class Ono and Yasui, learning to row in our boat, were two years younger than I was when I enrolled at the Naval Academy. They had to row in pairs before getting the knack of rowing single, and I sympathized with them in their diligent work and their exhaustion.

No one can master oarsmanship only by listening to others explain how to do it. It must be acquired as one's hands become blistered from rowing, as the skin peels from one's seat, and, more often than not, as one weeps inwardly.

Ono and Yasui, I thought, you are not the only ones suffering from the toil of rowing. Every sailor has learned it the hard way and in tears. Have patience for a while, and keep at it!

20

August 22
Into Nature's Bosom

"Hey, doggone it, my watch has stopped!" someone shrieked suddenly. Similar cries arose here and there in the boat. I immediately looked at my watch, and found that it had also stopped. I shook my left arm vigorously, but the hands of my watch did not move.

In those days our watches were not a hundred percent waterproof, so we knew very well they would stop sooner or later after being soaked in the seawater. Now that it had happened, we felt uneasy about the consequences.

A few days ago, the assistant navigator had announced, "As far as navigation of this boat unit goes, you don't have a thing to worry about, so long as we have a watch." The men who had heard this remark were startled, because the watches they had counted on had stopped. Up to then, we, the officers, had based our estimate of the distance covered during the night on the number of hours we had rowed, how skillfully we had rowed, and whether the winds had been favorable or unfavorable. So while we had regarded watches as a convenience, they were not essential. However, it was difficult to convince the enlisted men that this was true.

A few days before this, I had an experience regarding a watch that made a lasting impression on me. Shortly after noon during a time of inactivity, Seaman First Class Yamada, in the No. 3 boat, made a proposal to me. He said, "Mr. Matsunaga, I have a compass attached to my watchband. Please use it for navigation of our boats, sir."

"Everyone is taking a break now, Yamada," I said. "I'll borrow it from you later on when we get closer. Okay?"

Yamada must have thought that the sooner he turned it over to me, the sooner I could use it, so he threw his watch toward our boat, about ten meters from his. Unfortunately, it did not reach us, and fell into the sea. Yamada looked very regretful for this mishap.

Later that day, the senior officer talked to me about the incident.

"Mr. Matsunaga, I know the compass attached to a watchband has so little magnetic flux that it would be of no use in navigation. However, Yamada firmly believed that it would be helpful, and tried to turn it over to you immediately. By not responding right away, you trampled on his feelings and on his efforts to help.

"In normal naval duties, officers can expect obedience from their subordinates without regard for their feelings. But you must remember, even though we are still in the navy, the men are not getting enough food and rest. Under these circumstances, if the officers give orders, without consideration for their subordinates' feelings, it could lead to a mutiny somewhere along the line. From now on, I want you to remember not to hurt their feelings unnecessarily."

"Aye aye, sir. I will bear in mind what you have just said."

I had been thinking over how to explain the news to the crew that we could navigate successfully without a watch, when the assistant navigator spoke to me. "Mr. Matsunaga, our watches have stopped, but that will not adversely affect our voyage to the Philippines."

I leaned forward to listen to what he was going to say.

"By day, we can determine the time by the height of the sun from the horizon. At sunrise and sunset, its altitude is zero degrees. At noon its altitude is about eighty-six degrees. When the sun's altitude is forty-five degrees in the eastern sky, it is about three hours after sunrise. By the same token, when its altitude is forty-five degrees in the western sky, it is three hours before sunset.

"By night, we can avail ourselves of Cassiopeia and the Big Bear. These stars rotate counterclockwise around Polaris. By observing their location at sunset, and considering Polaris the center of the dial of a watch, we can easily estimate time in three-hour intervals. So you see, we can navigate successfully without a watch, sir."

"Mr. Hoshino, your explanation is very convincing. You're a born navigator. Let us go by your theory. Thank you."

As Ono listened to our conversation, it was evident that he also had great trust in the assistant navigator, who spoke with complete confidence.

Until now, our watches had been useful not only for telling time but also for navigation, for we calculated how far we had gone by observing the time difference of sunrise and sunset each day. Now we had to estimate the distance traveled from how effectively we rowed, and the time by observing the sun or stars. The assistant navigator realized that the crew might not understand this, and he wisely did not mention distance all that day. Though he was only twenty-one years old, he was wise enough to know what to say and when to be silent. He had become a top-notch naval officer.

Though a watch was not necessary for this voyage, to me it was a turning point of the situation. Until now the boat unit had been related to human society through our watches, but when they stopped, it was a loss of relationship with human society. From this moment on, we would depend solely on the relative movement of the sun, the stars, and the earth. It seemed to me that the senior officer was also pessimistic about the turn of events.

When I had a chance to talk with him alone at the stern, I whispered, "Senior Officer, our watches have stopped and we have lost our association with human society. I'm feeling rather discouraged."

"Mr. Matsunaga, my opinion is different from yours," he said. "Look, the crew has become tired. If our watches were still functioning, we would stick to a schedule and force them to work. The stopping of the watches indicates we need to break our association with human society and jump into Nature's bosom. Don't be down in the dumps about it. Cheer up!"

I noticed all along that the senior officer accepted the series of difficult events as the given conditions, and carefully considered not only how to cope with them but also how the men would be affected by his actions. For example, on the first night, when we rowed in pairs for the first time, ordinary officers would have reprimanded the crew for not having bent to the oars. Instead, he gave them kind advice.

From what he said on that night, I guessed that the senior officer was trying to keep up the men's morale by letting them know that he was optimistic about the situation. His words were fine in themselves, but I still had some reservations. He said we were cutting our relationship with human society and jumping into Nature's bosom. But weren't we jumping into Nature's bosom to reach our destination–human society?

It seemed to me that our determination to reach human society proved that we are social beings and, also, that we human beings have a deep desire to have our own death recognized by many others.

21

August 22
From Petty Officer Yamamoto's Story

When Yeoman First Class Ginji Yamamoto was pulled out of the water on the morning of August 20, he lost consciousness for a while. Although he was in good physical condition, he was completely exhausted after spending two days on a raft in the raging sea. Now he had recovered his strength, and was talking to his fellow crew members.

"I was born and raised in a small fishing village in Niigata prefecture, so I was a lot more familiar with the sea than those brought up inland. I knew that open seawater is very cold, so I told the men in my department to have on two sets of fatigues before jumping into the sea.

"Soon after we were in the water, a man came flying out of the water. I recognized him as Petty Officer Miyoji Anzai. What apparently happened is this. When a ship sinks below the surface, a huge mass of air remains in the hull. As the ship sinks to greater depths, the pressure of this air becomes so great that the hull finally ruptures. Obviously Petty Officer Anzai was blown out of the water enveloped in the compressed air.

"That first night, about ten men were on a raft. As the senior enlisted man in this group, I advised them not to waste their energy, but the sea was so rough that it was almost impossible for them to follow my advice. As the raft took a list to forward, everyone started moving aft. Then the raft began to list aft, and we had to move forward. We got very tired from moving back and forth so often. At times the raft was capsized by big swells, and we were thrown into the water, and almost every time the raft turned over, one of the men was carried away by the waves and disappeared into the dark sea. I felt very sorry for them, but under the circumstances, all I could do was try to save my own life. There was no way I could lend them a hand to get them back on the raft.

"On the second day, the sea raged fearfully all day long. That night, I saw an object that looked like a bar glimmering pale in the dark sea. I thought it was the drive shaft of the capsized launch, so I wanted, if at all possible, to get it aboard. To my great surprise, suddenly the object moved very swiftly. Then I realized that it was a man–eating shark.

"Petty Officer Seizaburo Kiyono, who was with me on the raft, had a piece of bleached cloth about two meters long coiled around his body. He immediately untied it, tore about ten centimeters off it, and tied his empty water canteen to its end. When the shark neared us for the second time, he calculated the timing, and threw the canteen on the surface of the water. The shark bit at it greedily and never came back."

Petty Officer Yamamoto then asked a young sailor sitting near him if he was a hospital man. Hospital Man Akazaki must have thought Petty Officer Yamamoto was going to reprimand him, and responded regretfully, "I am, sir. The chief petty officer of my department told me to abandon ship and go to the boat."

Petty Officer Yamamoto merely said okay and did not question him anymore. Akazaki had such an innocent face that he must have been a *tokunen hei*, a boy sailor who enlisted in the navy at the age of fourteen. Looking at Akazaki, who was giving a sigh of relief, I recalled that when the *Natori* was gradually going down, all the members of the medical corps department, directed by the medical corps officer, Surgeon Lieutenant Yoshimura, were busily engaged in transferring the wounded to the No. 2 launch. Though the chief petty officer of the medical corps department wanted everyone in his department to stay aboard and perform his assignment, he probably decided that at least the boy sailor, Akazaki, should be allowed to abandon ship.

I was surprised that the crusty chief petty officer had such compassion, and so that his kindness would not be wasted, I was determined to take Akazaki to land.

Stocker Petty Officer Motoharu Izu told a funny story. While he was swimming in the water after the *Natori* had gone down, he noticed a rat perching on his head. There is an old saying that a rat foresees disaster, so he told the men around him in the water that the rat had relied on him, which meant that whoever was with him would not die.

On the fourth day we saw, at a distance, something splashing in the water. As we neared it, we wondered if it was someone swimming or a fish. It turned out to be one of our crew members, Stocker Petty Officer Yoshidomi of the seventh department. We pulled him out of the water and laid him in the boat. It did not seem possible that he had been swimming for four days, but he had certainly been in the water for a terribly long time. He was completely exhausted.

When we got him on board and called his name, he responded by merely saying, "Ah..." and that was his dying word. We decided to bury him at sea. Stocker Petty Officer Masanao Chudo of the same department looked after his deceased buddy and said poignantly to me, "Yoshidomi was from Niigata prefecture. He was a married man, sir."

22

August 22
Health, Food, Water,
and Seniors of the Navy

Most of the crew experienced severe eye irritation from swimming after the *Natori* had gone to the bottom, because a film of
heavy oil covered the surface of the sea. Fortunately, it was cloudy
for the first two days, and the symptoms did not worsen. By the
third day, no one complained of throbbing pains in their eyes.

Five men who had suffered serious burns from the explosion
of the torpedo were in bad shape and died within the first few days.
They had extensive third-degree burns, and even if we had the
needed medical supplies there was nothing we could have done.

High winds day and night constantly covered us with spray of
seawater, which made us concerned about inflammation of the skin.
These worries soon passed, however, when we began encountering
alternate sunshine and rainsqualls.

When we began the heavy labor of rowing ten hours each day
with inadequate food, we were concerned about the health of the
men. This situation was compounded by the extremes of heat and
cold, lack of clothing or shelter to protect ourselves, and the crowded conditions in the boat. We decided that worrying too much
could itself have a negative effect, so we stopped worrying about
diseases we might contract in the future.

Fortunately, our voyage occurred during the rainy season in
the Philippine waters, and we had a rainsquall at least once a day,

which provided us with heaven-sent drinking water. After spending a few days at sea, it was easy to sight a rainsquall at a distance. As we entered the squall we would feel the blast of cold, gusty winds that always blew at the head of a rainsquall. Whenever we encountered these winds, we would stop rowing, put the oars in the boat, and take advantage of the rain.

At the beginning of the voyage, everyone tried to drink the rain simply by opening his mouth wide and catching the rain. But no matter how heavy the downpour was, the amount of water we could drink this way was never enough.

Then one smart seaman developed the technique of spreading out a towel with his hands and holding it centered between his teeth. It worked, and soon everyone imitated him. The towels smelled of sweat and oil, but we couldn't care less. A clean towel was too much to ask under the circumstances. Because no one could guarantee a rainsquall on the following day, we always drank appreciatively, as though it were as tasty as nectar.

During one heavy rainsquall I noticed that the boat was flooding with rainwater. We were already overloaded and had very little freeboard, so we had to take prompt action. I immediately passed the word, "Stop drinking rainwater. All hands, bail the water out. Bear a hand!"

There was no gear at all for bailing, so they began scooping the water with their hands. However, they had to move slowly, to avoid banging their hands on the hull or thwarts. A lot of water was slipping through their fingers, so I shouted, "Is bilge water decreasing or increasing?"

"Increasing, sir!" someone replied with a worried tone.

"Hear this," I said. "Unless we do better, the boat will go down. Bail the boat speedily!" Then someone called out, "Men, use your cap or rubber boots. You can scoop a lot of water with them." Their caps and rubber boots proved good bailers, and soon we got through the crisis.

I always had looked down on the regular navy bailer as ugly, heavy, and poorly designed, but after our experience, I realized that it was designed to protect our hands and fingers while bailing water, and that our seniors in the navy had developed a masterful design.

Unfortunately the bailers had not been stowed in the boats, but in the operations department storeroom. If God had allowed me to have but one piece of gear, I would, without hesitation, have asked for a bailer. Because there were no bailers in the boat, and no water in the water breakers, I grumbled when we officers shot the breeze.

"I know for a fact that the water breakers were filled on the ship. But when we went to use them they were empty. Why were they empty? Because they were made into oval cylinders and bound with loose hoops, and therefore leaked. If they had been made in a cylindrical shape, and bound tightly with hoops, it would have been much easier to make them, and the water would not have leaked out. Why did the seniors in the navy make such decisions?"

The senior officer responded to my remark. "Mr. Matsunaga, if the water breakers were a cylindrical shape, whether empty or full, they would be unstable and roll all over the place. Although they were well aware that the oval-shaped ones cost more and take more time to make, our seniors in the navy purposely made them into this shape. These water breakers are made of wood. After the wood has absorbed enough water, I'm sure they will serve their purpose."

Within a few days, the water breakers stopped leaking as the senior officer had predicted. Then I remembered the words he had spoken a few days ago.

"You should remember, our voyage is backed by a great many seniors of the navy who are warmly watching over us."

As we experienced many hardships in a boat far out in the Pacific Ocean, I realized that the things the seniors in the navy had developed were remarkably dependable in emergencies.

23

August 22
Dealing with the Crews
in Their Extremity

When abandoning the *Natori*, I carried a short sword with me, which I had concealed under my jacket. Here is why. When Japanese naval officers sailed from the homeland, they brought a sword aboard, presumably, to be prepared to command a landing party, though it may also have been to carry on the tradition of the samurais, who took a sword with them to the battlefield.

When our ship *Furutaka* sank, I swam with a sword tied on my back, which made swimming exceptionally hard work. It took me a good half hour to swim to the rescue vessel only a thousand meters away, and I became thoroughly exhausted. Since then, I always carried this short sword.

One day I stood on the stern sheets of our boat, showing this short sword to the men, and said, "Hear this. I think the U.S. Navy is trying to locate our boats to capture the officers, because we have information they want. When they come to get us, I want you men to sit tight and stay calm. Remember, I have this short sword, and they won't take me without a fight."

Although I implied I would use my sword to protect myself, I really wanted them to realize that I would use it to deal with anyone who would steal provisions or attempt a mutiny.

There was another important issue. A machine gun had been set at the bow, and if the crew had mutinied and pointed a machine gun at my breast, I couldn't possibly confront them with my short sword. So, I suggested to the senior officer to have the machine gun moved to the stern. He thought carefully before responding. "The machine gun is set at the bow to enable us to protect ourselves from attackers. The only reason to move it to the stern is to protect the officers against rebellion. But we are only four officers against sixty enlisted men. In case of a mutiny, we won't have a chance, and would all be killed anyhow. Leave the machine gun at the bow as it is."

What we needed was a sense of mutual reliance and trust between the officers and the enlisted men, which was not something that came naturally or could simply be handed to us. It had to be created bit by bit through communication between the parties. There was no other way.

In our extreme circumstances, insincere flattery was as bad as speaking harshly or insulting the person, and would quickly destroy a sense of trust. I never thought so seriously about choosing appropriate words as I did during this voyage. The senior officer told the officers, "I don't want any of you to say anything that may discourage the men. You should never tell a lie or deceive them."

I was reminded that when a patient lies between life and death, his doctor never makes a pessimistic remark to the patient or the patient's family. I felt that the possibility of success on this voyage was far less than that of failure. But if I told this to the crew, they would take a pessimistic view of the situation. So, to be honest without discouraging them, I had to select each word very carefully, and talk to them as a doctor does to his patients.

Each evening, before the rowing began, the senior officer brought the boats together and spoke to the men. He passed on all the information he had and his best judgment of the situation. This showed his zeal and sincerity in making decisions, thereby making a profound impression on the men who listened to him.

Given the arduous task of rowing, the limited supply of food and water, the extremes of heat and cold, the crowded conditions in the boat, and the fact that our success was not assured, a rebellion by the crew was certainly a possibility. I believe that one reason they did not mutiny was the wisdom, demeanor, and tact of the senior officer, and another was that the rations were given equally to everyone, irrespective of status, rank, or rating.

24

August 22
Diversions

Experiences I had in previous years and conversations with men in the boat made me realize that people carry over skills from their early environment to live. So, one day I said to Mr. Yamashita, who had been born and bred by the sea, "Hey, Number Nine, I understand you are from a fishing village, and therefore you must know how to live by the sea. There must be some other men here who grew up by the sea. Let's get them together and organize a fishing squad, with you as the leader. What do you think?"

I had already obtained permission from the senior officer to implement this idea. "Hear this," I said. "We are going to organize a fishing squad with those born and brought up by the sea. Mr. Yamashita will be the leader. With your background, I am confident you know how to live by the sea. Now use your abilities for the common good. Whether you are a senior or a junior, speak out what you have known or noticed that will help you carry out this job. Is that clear?"

As I passed the word to organize a fishing squad, five men responded. Sailors frequently stuck a threaded needle in their caps, so that it would be available at a moment's notice, and in the end we were given three needles to be made into fishhooks. Petty Officer Sato, a fisherman in civilian life, would be in charge of the task.

The men working on the fishing project in the third boat

snapped two sewing needles while trying to bend them into a fish-hook, but then someone suggested that a needle would not snap while being bent if it was preheated. They preheated the one remaining needle by rubbing it against the barrel of the machine gun, and were able to bend it into a fishhook. Then they twisted white thread into a cord, and kneaded crumbs for bait.

They wasted no time in casting a line. Although we saw fish in the water, they would not take the bait of crumbs. Others also tried fishing from the second boat, but without success. We had placed great hope in fishing, but we finally had to give it up.

Then I recalled a lecture on oceanography at the Naval Academy and passed a new challenge on to the fishing squad: "When I studied oceanography at the Naval Academy I learned that the seawater forty meters below the surface has less salt content than that near the surface. Everyone in the boats is dying for drinking water, so let's see if there is a way to scoop up water with less salt content for everyone to drink."

Petty Officer Second Class Kimura replied immediately. "Beg pardon, Mr. Matsunaga, it's a piece of cake. A favorite expression of my grandfather was, when you have encountered a disaster at sea, scoop up water at twenty fathoms below the surface and drink it. Twenty fathoms is almost the same as forty meters. In grandpa's tale, he would use an *one-sho* bottle [a container for Japanese sake, or rice wine]. There are no *one-sho* bottles in the boat, so let's try the cider bottles instead, okay, sir?"

My idea in suggesting this assignment for the fishing squad was not so much to scoop water as to play for time by diverting their attention, for they were very much concerned about whether or not rescue ships would come to our aid. I was quite taken aback by the prompt answer, for I thought the assignment would take some time. At any rate, because the theory I learned at the Naval Academy concurred with the fisherman's practical know-how, we decided to give it a try.

Three empty cider bottles were in our boat and for a line we unwound a piece of cord coiled around an oar (it was coiled to prevent the oar from being worn out by friction with the oarlock). For a weight to attach to the bottles, we decided to use a sling shackle. The idea was to fasten one end of the line, about forty meters long, to an empty bottle. The line was wound in such a way that a plug was made of the line, which was inserted into the mouth of the bottle, and the weight was fastened to the bottle, so that it would sink slowly into the sea. When the bottle was forty meters below the surface, the line was jerked pulling the plug out of the mouth of the bottle. The bottle, filled with water, would then be pulled slowly to the surface.

The task did not go as easily as we had expected. The cider bottles seemed to be suitable, but we couldn't find the right weight to match the buoyancy of the bottle. When the weight was too light, the cider bottle would float sideways on the surface. If the weight was too heavy, the bottle was pulled into the water too quickly. Also, the line tended to curl, which contributed to our failure. After having tried this and that, we lost two of the three bottles.

Almost all the other crew members were engrossed in watching how the task was done, and talking about nothing but the progress of the task, forgetting all their worries about the future. Although we had failed in the specific task, at least it was a good distraction.

I decided to discontinue the task and save the last cider bottle, because I had a definite purpose in mind. If the time came when reaching shore seemed hopeless, I would put a message into the bottle and cast it on the ocean, in the hope that it would be found and read. I had been instructed by the senior officer not to mention a word that might discourage the men, so I could not disclose my plan to anyone, not even to Mr. Yamashita.

PART SEVEN

ROWING

25

August 23
Mr. Yamashita's Real Intent

On August 23, our sixth day at sea, I had an important discussion with the senior officer. On navy units as well as at the Naval Academy, it was standard practice for old-timers to give an *o-tasshi*, or scolding, to their juniors and to stimulate them to action. Because I felt this need, I requested the senior officer to give an *o-tasshi*, but he refused, stating that a scolding was effective only for an hour or so at the most, and therefore might do more harm than good.

I could think of no other way to encourage the men, so I asked the senior officer how we were going to command and lead the men. He replied: "Mr. Matsunaga, a proverb says, `Sincerity moves heaven.' I believe if we officers treat the men from our hearts and souls, they will respond to us."

This was true, but another proverb says, "Well fed, well bred." Under our adverse living conditions, I was not sure the men would respond to the commanding officer's sincerity.

Although I did not oppose the senior officer's opinion openly, I was not persuaded by his words either. I believed our problems were far more profound than could be handled by such a simple approach. The senior officer, as though reading my mind, added this comment:

"On board ship, officers frequently crack jokes with enlisted men. As long as everyone realizes these are jokes, there will not be any problem. But the jokes can readily cause a misunderstanding between the officers and enlisted men, and if that occurs repeatedly, the officers will lose the confidence and respect of their men. From now on we will have to select each word carefully. Incidentally, Mr. Matsunaga, I want you to think out a daily order to be maintained in the boats."

As is customary when receiving an order from one's superior, I reflectively repeated and accepted his order. However, I did not have the slightest idea as to the specific order that should be maintained in the boats. Then, I selected the words "discipline" and "rules" as synonyms of the word "order," and tried to analyze what he meant.

I was really at my wit's end, when Mr. Yamashita suggested to me that we introduce a new rhythm and tempo into the routine life in the boats. He expanded his thoughts along this line, saying that when we were on the ship, the daily routine, such as rising, meals, and standing watch, were scheduled so that everyone knew what to expect and was ready for it. In the boat, however, no such routines had been established, which more or less kept everyone on standby at all times. If things continued this way, we would soon be all tired out. What we needed to do was to establish daily routines.

"Thanks, Number Nine. The senior officer has just given me an assignment to establish the new order in the boat, but I have not been able to figure out a specific plan. Your idea is thought-provoking. I will establish a daily routine right away. If you have any other ideas, don't hesitate to let me know. I surely appreciate it."

"Mr. Matsunaga, I have always been under the impression that in the navy, the line officers are the most important and the others take backseats. I'm impressed that you immediately adopted my suggestion. Thank you, Mr. Matsunaga."

"Number Nine, I guess the reason the senior officer assigned you to this leading boat was that he wanted to take advantage of your expertise. Because you were bred by the sea, you have something we landlubbers don't have. This additional strength makes a great contribution to our outfit. Further, we Naval Academy graduates are apt to think that enlisted men will act only if we tell them to, but your training in the Higher Merchant Marine School taught you how to create an environment in which they will work better. I am grateful for your efforts. Say, Number Nine, you and I are about the same age. Why don't we call each other by `kisama' and `ore' (navy jargon used among familiar friends)?"

I held out my hand, and firmly shook his to indicate that my words were not just a compliment, but that I really meant what I said, and to let him know that I was relying on him. I then told him my reasoning. "When I was a green ensign aboard the battleship *Haruna* as junior first lieutenant, Engr. Lt. Yoshizo Watanabe was in the same wardroom. He was a graduate of the Kobe Higher Merchant Marine School, and a good drinker and good conversationalist. One time he pointed out an important difference between the navy and the merchant marine.

"In the navy, when an officer passes the word, the petty officers decide how to get the work done and then direct sailors to do it. However, on a merchant ship no personnel correspond to petty officers in the navy. Therefore, an engineering officer on a merchant ship passes the word directly to the firemen, who are equivalent to sailors of the navy. His orders must not require any judgment on the part of the firemen, but must be simple and direct, and as much work as possible must be incorporated into a daily work routine. Because I had this background knowledge about the merchant marine, I felt like adopting your timely suggestion right off the bat."

The senior officer served as a navigator during peacetime for such a long time that he associated sunrise and sunset with his sextant observations, and could enjoy the beauty of sunset and sunrise. But the war broke out soon after my graduation from the Naval Academy, and so, at sunset the first thing that always came to my mind was to be on guard against enemy submarines. And I was always so tight and tense that I never really enjoyed the beauty of the setting sun when I was on board ship.

Now, living in a boat out in the vast ocean, I could truly enjoy the beauty of the setting sun. I realized that Nature was far more beautiful and vivid than any picture I had ever seen. This was a wonderful serendipity of a demanding, difficult voyage.

26

August 24
Illusions, Recreation,
and Conversations

An issue arose that became difficult for the officers. Every so often men would say, "We see an island over there, let's make for it."

Did they say this because of wishful thinking or was there a visual illusion? Sometimes stationary clouds just above the horizon prompted their suggestions, but knowing where the *Natori* had gone down, and the distance we had covered so far, it was impossible that land would be in sight. So, no matter how earnestly they asked that we head for the perceived island, the senior officer never granted their request.

On one occasion the man who had made the request and the senior officer looked at each other with anger in their eyes. Instantly invisible, but intense, sparks flew between them, as the man openly and rudely opposed his superior.

This led me to evaluate the current attitude and psychological condition of the men, and as I did so it seemed to me the crew was looking sterner each day. I observed this especially among the petty officers, in the bow of the boat. Did these changes in their facial expression and general demeanor result from having lost much of their vigor, or from an accumulation of complaints? Also, it seemed to me that there was more whispering among the petty officers than before. If they wanted to revolt against the officers, the group of sailors between us would serve as a shield, and I was beginning to worry again about the machine gun in the bow.

Then, as the second boat approached us, I looked carefully at the special service torpedo officer and the paymaster, and realized that the expressions on their faces were different from usual. The special service torpedo officer, in his forties, who always had a gentle look, had sunken cheeks and a stern look; the paymaster, in his twenties, did not look so hollow-eyed, but there were shadows under his eyes. Then I noticed that the young sailors, in their teens, still had roundish cheeks. I began to realize that the sterner looks of the petty officers were, after all, primarily a reflection of their age.

Thus I realized anew that if we officers distrusted the men, and they did not have confidence in us, we would not achieve our goal. I resolved not to be suspicious of them, and to be very careful in speaking to them that I did not, in any way, berate them. Through the stern looks of the petty officers, God had reminded me to treat the men with consideration and kindness.

I now became concerned about our eyesight. Because we had been and would be doing the heavy labor of rowing ten hours a day with limited nutrition, it was possible that we would all become night-blinded. One of the greatest tragedies of a disaster at sea is that survivors cannot recognize land even though it is right before their eyes. To avoid this tragedy, I thought that at least one of us should take precautionary measures to avoid night blindness.

Fortunately, I had at hand a few small cans of condensed milk besides the regular ration of ship's biscuits. It was not enough for all hands, but would maintain physical strength of one person. Then I suggested to the senior officer that he consume it for the sake of the boat unit. He turned down my suggestion, for he was unwilling to eat more than the other men. How fortunate we were to have as the senior officer a young man, twenty-seven years old, strong and vigorous physically, who had a good command of the art of navigation.

Though the first two days after the *Natori* sank were cloudy and overcast, each of the following days was sunny and hot. Even with the shelter we erected, the men were very uncomfortable in the crowded boats. As their discomfort increased with each passing day, the crew persistently requested permission to have a dip in the sea.

At first I denied the request, believing that we should conserve all our strength for the difficult task of rowing three hundred miles in fifteen days with a minimal supply of food; yet I thought it was important to listen to the men, particularly when we did not heed them when they reported seeing islands. Therefore, I decided to give this a try. Keeping my fatigues on for fear of sharks, I descended into the water while holding onto a painter tied to the stern.

The moment I was in the sea I relaxed, and the stress and tension I was experiencing were eased to a remarkable degree. The buoyancy of the water seemed to buoy my spirit as well as my body, and I was revived physically as well as psychologically.

At first I continued to grip the painter, for, having eaten very little for six days, I was not sure I could swim. Then I let go of the painter and moved my arms and legs very slowly, and found I could keep myself afloat. As I moved my arms and legs freely, the pain in my joints, which had become severe in the cramped conditions of the boat, disappeared. Though I had exerted some physical energy, I felt that I had gained far more than I had lost.

Back in the boat, I reported to the senior officer. "Sir, after I was in the water, it really eased my aches and renewed my spirit. I recommend that the men be allowed to have a dip in the sea."

Beginning that day we took turns, and each man had a five-minute dip every day, which proved to be a wonderful recreation for the crew. After a dip, we wrapped ourselves in our fatigues. Though these became soaking wet with seawater, the salinity was washed away by the daily rainsqualls.

One day someone in the water near the boat cried with joy, "Hey, I caught crabs and ate them!"

Others then dove into the water, and found very small crabs clinging to the bottom of the boat, and gave me three of them. They were as tiny as grains of rice, and as far as nutrition was concerned, the amount was trifling. But I ate a living thing for the first time in a long time, and felt as though a new vital power were flowing in my body. These tiny crabs became a popular topic for the men to shoot the breeze about.

The daily assembly of the boats allowed the men to converse with persons in the other boats, and this also became a welcome part of each day's activities. On the day I took my first dip, I began a conversation with an ensign in the third boat, and was impressed by the fact that he was rowing at one of the middle oars, sharing in our hardship. He said his name was Shozawa and that he was a graduate of Tokyo Imperial University and had completed a reserve officers course. He had taken passage on the *Natori* to his new duty station, the air defense unit on Palau Island.

As we conversed we realized that we had a common friend in Paymaster Lt. (jg) Koichi Hayashi, a former shipmate of mine who was also a graduate of Tokyo Imperial University. I recalled that one day Mr. Hayashi had spoken kindly to me with these words: "Mr. Masunaga, you are destined to become a commanding officer some day. In this wide world, there are those who excel in scholastic abilities, and others who lead all the rest in physical strength. But you have both superior scholastic ability and physical strength. I want you to proceed on your way to becoming a commanding officer with pride and confidence."

In response to Lieutenant Hayashi's encouragement and Ensign Shozawa's cooperation, I renewed my resolve to fulfill my responsibilities as the second in command of the boat unit to the best of my ability.

I was especially touched by one series of conversations as the boats were together. Leading Seaman Ichiro Takahashi was a graduate of a teachers college and worked a short time as a teacher before he was drafted into the navy. Ex-teachers who were drafted were called *shichos*. These men were very proficient in clerical duties and were valued members of ships crews. Several other *shichos* were in the boats, and when the boats assembled, these men enjoyed talking together and reminiscing about their experiences as teachers. I was especially impressed by Takahashi's frequent references to his former pupils and his concern for them. I realized anew that teaching truly is a noble profession.

It was good that our thoughts and aspirations could go beyond our present situation to the things that brought fulfillment and purpose to our lives.

27

August 25
A Secret of Command
and Leadership

Leading Seaman Saburo Wakamatsu, in the second boat, and Seaman First Class Tamotsu Takeuchi, in the third boat, died from fatigue on August 25. They had been adrift on a raft for such a long time and were so exhausted that they had simply lain on the bottom of the boat, hoping to recover, but never did. After sundown, we had an informal religious service and buried them at sea. This was the first time that two men, other than those who had been burned, died on the same day, and there was a great sadness. I hoped that their death would not have a disheartening effect on the crew's morale.

I now reflected on what it means to command and evaluated the senior officer's leadership skills. I remembered that the course on command at the Naval Academy began with this lecture:

"To command means to concentrate the physical and mental strength and the technical ability of subordinates upon a single objective. According to an old statement, 'One cannot take the bull by the horns without expert knowledge in one's profession.' Therefore, you must always study and work hard to become an expert in knowledge and leadership. Then, in case of an emergency, you will be able to cut the Gordian knot with clear presence of mind. The secret of command is to learn from your own experiences throughout life, and not simply read about others."

We were also taught that during a war against an enemy, situations might develop when officers had to send their men into the jaws of death. Thus, officers must develop attitudes of mind and heart that earned their men's respect and dependence, and the men should also be willing to take orders, even to possible death. After such lectures, however, I did not feel like I had acquired the ability to command like this.

After being commissioned as ensign, I was attached to the battleship *Haruna* as junior first lieutenant. On this occasion my father, Sadaichi Matsunaga, a rear admiral, sent me a reference book about command; it was a Japanese translation of a book on command in naval vessels for midshipmen at Annapolis, written by a U. S. admiral. In a section about primitive instincts and desires of human beings, it stressed that to command effectively, they could not be ignored.

According to the book, man's strongest desire was thirst, and cold water should always be available to the men. With this in mind, I made a tour of the crew's quarters on the *Haruna*, and was surprised to find that every teakettle was empty in an effort to conserve fresh water. I then talked with one of the engineering officers and arranged for drinking water to be available in the crew's quarters at all times. Although it was far from the ideal of cold water, at least the crew was no longer in want of drinking water.

The book went on to state that when special duties, such as loading perishables or boats, had to be carried out during a mealtime, those assigned to this detail should be allowed to eat early. No one minded having a meal before others, but doing heavy work during mealtime on an empty stomach created discontent and increased the likelihood of accidents. Therefore, whenever possible, those assigned to such details on our ship ate before working.

The manual about the American way of exercising command was helpful to a first lieutenant. Yet even this book did not suggest on how to command when men had to perform heavy labor for more than ten days with insufficient food, sleep, and rest. I was utterly in the dark about how to command the crew under such an emergency situation.

Officers' uniforms, when we were on board ship, were different from those of enlisted men, and there were battle stations at which officers exercised special authority. In the boat, however, there was no battle station for the senior officer to show his authority, and his uniform was just as dirty as the crew's.

Although no means of controlling the crew had been taken

over the seven days since the disaster, military discipline had been well maintained, and the boats were making their way to the Philippines slowly but steadily as planned. If the crew had been rowing against their will, the boats could not have covered the distance according to the plan. The *Natori* boat unit was certainly receiving excellent command from the senior officer, and I began to consider how he had accomplished this.

First of all, the senior officer was an expert in the art of navigation, not just in theory, but also in conning a ship. The commanding officer of the *Natori* had relied on him and he was greatly respected by the crew. Second, in the boat he always assumed a resolute attitude, and never behaved as if he were tired or in difficulty.

The senior officer had been an outstanding judo player in Niigata High School, and at the Naval Academy he was one of the top five judo players among the one thousand midshipmen. He even had won the Squadron Judo Tournament. His outstanding physical strength raised the morale of the crew of the boat unit, even though no one mentioned it.

Among officers, there were always some who worked hard only when the commanding or executive officer was around, or were meekly obedient to their superiors but lorded it over the rank and file. The senior officer, however, was known as one who treated his superiors and subordinates the same and with sincerity.

Lt. Comdr. Rikihei Inoguchi, an instructor in the sciences of command and leadership, once told us, "If you wait until after an emergency occurs to start exercising command over your men, you will surely find it too late, no matter how hard you try. To command men skillfully in an emergency, you must always have the respect and trust of your subordinates."

On the previous night we had made our formation for night navigation, mooring the three boats in a line and rowing as usual. After midnight, however, the sea became so rough that we could not proceed as planned. Each boat then dragged its sea anchor and drifted until the stormy weather was over.

In the morning, the second boat was not too far away from us, but the third boat was nowhere to be seen. We decided, before anything else, to go and find it, setting up an oar as a mast and hoisting an ensign at its top. When we used sea anchors two nights ago, the third boat had drifted a good distance leeward by the following morning. So we decided to search that way first.

We had rowed for about twenty minutes when the lookout shouted, "One mast, right twenty degrees, two zero," meaning that he sighted a mast at twenty degrees to our right at two thousand meters. As we neared it, it proved to be the third boat. Whenever we dragged a sea anchor, I noticed that the third boat always drift-ed farther downwind than the other two boats, and I suspected there must be a reason.

After we were ashore, I asked Petty Officer Hashimoto, the bowman in the third boat, about it. He admitted that on the day of the disaster he happened to be at the bow of the third boat, and therefore was the one to make a sea anchor. But because he had long ago forgotten how to make bowline knots, he tied a sling improperly to the log. When he later pulled the sea anchor out of the water, he found the sling was gone, and from then on, he had to depend on a defective sea anchor, for it had no weight. Fortunately nothing serious happened because of that defective sea anchor.

28

August 26
Hopes and Disappointments

Our boat unit had already covered a good distance and we thought that we had about sixty more miles to go, so we expected to see some branches or materials floating in the water. However, we looked in vain and some of the men were beginning to wonder if we would ever reach shore. I was getting irritated myself.

Later on, when I thought about the situation calmly, I remembered that the North Equatorial Current flows westward in this area, so, even though we were getting closer to the Philippines, there was no reason to encounter floating materials drifting west to east against the current. I was ashamed of myself for not thinking more clearly. After five years at sea, I was no more mature than an inexperienced seaman.

"One medium–attack bomber. Right fifty degrees, altitude forty degrees. Proceeding to the left!" The shout came from the lookout at the bow. It appeared that this medium–attack bomber, probably out of Tacloban airfield in the southern part of Luzon Island, had been patrolling the east waters of the Philippines, and was returning to its home base.

Those who had been lying on the bottom of the boat quickly got up, and the men stood up on the thwarts by turns. Some shouted at the top of their voice, and others waved their jackets, eager to have this plane spot them. But the plane disappeared in the western sky without having shown any response to us. We had such high expectations that our disappointment and discouragement were even greater than before.

Looking at the discouraged men, I thought about the supplies U.S. pilots had with them in case they were shot down and had to drift in a life raft: charts, a magnetic compass, rations, medical supplies, a fishing kit, a mirror, a flashlight, and a signal pistol. Not one of these items was in our boats. I was frustrated when I realized that if there had been a mirror in the boat, we could have reflected the sun's rays to the plane to attract the pilot's attention.

Among commanding officers, some stand on their dignity by condemning their higher headquarters, or by having their subordinates on the carpet. But the senior officer neither condemned the Fleet Headquarters in Manila because rescue ships had not yet arrived, nor became critical because the boats did not proceed as planned. He accepted the conditions as they were, quietly and diligently coping with them.

In this way he had a profound influence on the staff officers. Until a few days ago, we would complain, saying that we could have done this or that if we had such-and-such a gear. Now we followed the lead of the senior officer, and concentrated on doing our best with what we had. The crew's attitude also changed, and they worked to solve difficult situations without relying on others. Right after the disaster, their conversations consisted mostly of "When will the rescue ships come?" or "Are we going to be picked up?" But the rescue ships never came, and the friendly planes that flew over close to our boats did not recognize us. Despite this, they began to talk with confidence and hope.

Before our beginning to row on this day, the senior officer passed the following word to the crew: "It is only common sense that when an outfit encounters a disaster, whether on land or at sea, its power of resistance and fighting strength will decrease day by day. Instead, your strength and power have increased as time goes by.

"Right after the disaster, we were worrying that the boats might capsize in the storm. Now we have sea anchors. When the sea gets rough, all we have to do is to drag them and wait for the tropical depression to pass. At first, leakage was so bad in the water breakers that they were of no use, but now the leakage has stopped and we can store fresh water in them. On top of that, nothing is more delightful than to see how you have become accustomed to rowing in pairs. At the very beginning of this voyage, as you may recall, we did not progress half as much as planned. Now the distance we cover every day exceeds thirty miles.

"Although there are no landmarks to let us know how far we have come, you can rest assured that we have been steadily proceeding to the west, determining our direction from the stars. The planes we have seen so far all had two engines. But within a few days we will see single-engine planes flying over, which means that we are near land."

As the senior officer predicted, a small plane flew over us on the following day. Just as the previous planes failed to recognize us, this plane did not see us either. But this time the crew did not become disappointed. They realized that we were getting closer and closer to land, and at the same time, they put more trust in the senior officer.

29

August 26
Proposal for Maintaining
Military Discipline

The ninth division officer, Mr. Yamashita, asked me, "Mr. Matsunaga, you have a piece of white string tied around your finger. Is that a charm for something, sir?"

"Yes, there is quite a history behind it." Saying this, I took a photo out of the pocket of my jacket.

Looking at it Mr. Yamashita said, "I thought you said you were a bachelor, Mr. Matsunaga. I didn't expect that you had such a charming baby."

"Hey, Number Nine, you have this all wrong. The baby's name is Namio Takagi. He is a grandson of Vice Admiral Kenzo Itoh, the commandant of the 30th Naval Base in Palau." I then told him the story of my visit to the vice admiral's son-in-law, First Secretary Takagi, at the embassy in Manilla, and how sad I was that I could not deliver this photo.

The rainsqualls we encountered covered such a small area that depending on where the boats might be, one might benefit from the rain, while the others did not. One day when we were out of luck, the third boat voluntarily offered us three canteens full of water. Although we were very grateful to them for their kindness, we declined their offer, because we all knew that water was precious. When they said, "We have a water–gathering device in our boat, so don't be afraid to accept our offer," I was not only grateful for their offer, but also surprised at their practical ability in improvising such a contrivance.

Seaman First Class Taguchi, Mr. Kubo's orderly, had brought Mr. Kubo's raincoat with him into the third boat, and Warrant Officer Takabayashi and Petty Officer Kobayashi organized a water-gathering detail. Whenever they spotted a dark rainsquall, they would proceed to the area where it was raining, spread the raincoat to collect the water, and pour it into water canteens using a funnel made from an empty biscuit can.

On board ship, the officers lived in the wardroom quarters near the stern; the enlisted men had their quarters in the bow or amidship. Thus the officers and enlisted men didn't know one another well. In the boat, however, we literally lived elbow to elbow and under identical conditions. As a result, a new fraternization developed, and this, together with the increased confidence the enlisted men had in the officers, created a sense of camaraderie.

On one occasion, Seaman Second Class Ono spoke to the senior officer directly.

"Navigator, when do you think the rescue ships will be here, sir?"

"Ono, the situation has deteriorated to such an extent that I think that our headquarters in Manila cannot afford to dispatch rescue ships. Under the circumstances, we should not expect them to come to our aid."

Looking at Ono, who appeared unhappy, I asked myself if such familiarity should continue. On board ship it would never occur to a young sailor to speak directly to the captain. The captain lived in quarters all by himself, and his only duty station was the bridge. He was always neatly dressed, and assumed such a serious, aloof attitude that young sailors would not feel free to speak to him directly.

Lieutenant Kobayashi was the commanding officer of this outfit, so it was more appropriate to address him as senior officer than as navigator, even though he had no separate room for his own use, and his uniform was as dirty as ours. Under such circumstances, it might be too much to expect Ono, who was inexperienced, to address him as senior officer. Yet the downside to such fraternization and familiarity was that it could hinder the senior officer's ability to command.

Command and respect for authority were drilled into us in various ways at the Naval Academy as we learned "to draw the line." Midshipmen could not enter certain places during their first year at the Naval Academy, and they could not fraternize or have friendly conversations with upperclassmen. At first this was hard for me to accept, and some of my experiences were unpleasant, but after six months I understood and accepted the reason for this.

Seaman Second Class Ono was still young. If I had told him to draw the line, he would not have understood what this meant, and the good aspects of his fraternization with the senior officer would be completely destroyed. Was there a way in which I could eliminate undue familiarity without destroying the unity and harmony so essential to our mission? To do this the officers would have to set a good example for the enlisted men. Therefore, I spoke to Mr. Yamashita and Mr. Hoshino as follows:

"As you know, for over a week we have had limited food and water, insufficient rest, and we have been working hard at our rowing. Everyone is getting close to the point where he can barely exist. Nevertheless, we must have an environment in which everyone will absolutely obey the senior officer's orders.

"To have the crew fully understand what a commanding officer is, I want everyone to call him senior officer, not Lieutenant Kobayashi or navigator. Also, I don't want you two to speak to him directly. If there is something you want to talk to him about, I will be a go-between for you. Is that clear?"

Both nodded meekly. The senior officer, sitting only a meter away from us, must have heard my proposition clearly and I was well aware of his presence. He was placed in the most awkward position by my proposal, for this would set him on a pedestal.

From this moment on, he could no longer have informal conversations with officers or enlisted men. However, I shot the breeze with him for half an hour before the rowing began each night. For privacy we talked with our backs turned to the crew.

Within a few days after this new proposal was enforced, no one in our boat spoke directly to the senior officer. As time passed, everyone was becoming more irritated, and sometimes our feelings reached the boiling point, yet the steps we took helped maintain military discipline.

On this day, Leading Seamen Chikara Abe of the first boat and Shigeru Kurata of the third boat died from fatigue. Both had drifted on a raft for two days before being picked up by the boats, and they never recovered from exhaustion. After sundown, we buried them quietly at sea. Two crew members had also died the day before, and a somber mood prevailed over the entire boat unit.

At the boat officers' assembly that day, the senior officer

passed the following word: "We will hit the beach tomorrow morning. I want all hands in shipshape appearance. Keep a strict watch with the machine gun. Find out the name of the place immediately after landing."

These were very unexpected words from the senior officer, and Mr. Hoshino and I looked at each other in amazement. Judging from our estimate of the distance we had traveled so far, it seemed incredible that we would reach shore on the following morning; the senior officer, an expert in the art of navigation, must have been aware of this. We concluded that he must have said this to offset the somber atmosphere in the boat unit. He was also preparing us for the possibility of facing hostility from natives when we went ashore.

30

August 27
Some Ideas and Reflections
as We Neared Land

This was our tenth day at sea after the disaster. We knew we were nearing the eastern shores of the Philippines, and many of our thoughts and conversations revolved around this event, but we were tired and the task ahead loomed very large and difficult. We officers thought a good deal about how to encourage and inspire ourselves and the men.

During the Pacific War, the leaders of Japan tried to boost the nation's fighting spirit by utilizing the slogan *hakko-ichiu*. The concept behind this word, which can be translated "the-all-the-world-one-family principle," was abstract and not understood by most people. Many thought there should be a catchword that was easier to understand. In contrast, the slogan "Remember Pearl Harbor" was used in the United States, and even children could easily understand its meaning.

We officers wanted a slogan that would capture the crew's commitment as they set out on our journey. We did not have a common religious faith or taboos or a catchword, and those beliefs are not usually developed overnight. But we thought that somehow we could develop a catchword that would bring a sense of unity and purpose to our endeavors. But what would that slogan be?

That afternoon, while I was dozing under the shelter, I overheard Seamen Second Class Ono and Yasui say that they did not want to get lost on the way, a topic they had been talking about for the past few days. Judging from this, it seemed that a major theme of conversation had been, "We don't want to get lost."

It seemed to me that this obsession developed because of the monotony. Day in and day out, we saw nothing but the blue surface of the water and the sun shining in the cloudless sky. Each night we experienced the monotony of rowing for ten hours. Under such circumstances, the words "We don't want to get lost" ran through the mind of the crew, so I thought that the slogan "Don't get lost" captured the unity and purpose of the crew. From time to time we used that slogan to encourage one another.

We now began to see white birds occasionally, and I wondered if we could determine the direction of land by observing their flight paths. I had heard that in olden days seamen would carry birds with them in their ships. When they were uncertain of their directions, the birds were released, and the direction of land was indicated by their flight path. As I thought about this, I looked out and saw one of these white birds. Today I wished that it would keep company with us all day long. But alas, it flew toward us for only a moment and then flew away. Was there land in the direction in which it flew? I pondered this question.

We staff officers had a serious discussion about what signs would appear as we approached land. Mr. Yamashita said that we would see leaves of palm trees or pieces of wood floating in the water. I said that birds, such as kites and sea gulls, and small fish that live near the coast would make their appearance.

But that monarch of the sea, the Pacific Ocean, never let us see any evidences of land. I then recalled a phenomenon near land known as sea breeze and land breeze. During the day the air temperature over land is higher than over the water. As a result, the air pressure is less over land, and a cool breeze, called a sea breeze, blows inland from the sea. At night, when the temperature is higher over the sea, the flow is reversed, and a land breeze blows from land to sea. A lull occurs when the wind direction changes in the morning and in the evening.

"Mr. Hoshino, we should be able to perceive sea breeze and land breeze as we get close to land," I said.

"Sir, even if there were such phenomena, the wind velocity would be very low. Don't you think it would be impossible for us to perceive the breeze, Mr. Matsunaga?"

Then Mr. Yamashita spoke up. "Mr. Hoshino, when a fisherman wants to find the wind direction, he dips his finger into the sea, then holds it up. The side of his finger that dries first is the windward."

"That is quite logical, Mr. Yamashita, but setting that all aside, could we really expect to perceive sea breeze or land breeze here in this area? As you know, the Philippine Islands consist of over seven thousand islands. There are big islands, such as Luzon or Mindanao, all right, but most of them are so small that we shouldn't expect these phenomena to be present. So, I don't think we can determine our approach to land by detecting a sea breeze or land breeze, sir."

Then Mr. Yamashita made another suggestion. "When we near the land, we might be able to hear the sound of waves breaking on the shore, or smell the odors of land, Mr. Hoshino."

"We cannot expect to notice sounds or smell if winds are unfavorable. These phenomena could help us, but we cannot depend on them."

Then I spoke. "Mr. Hoshino, tell me, how will the land appear as we first gain sight of it?"

"Well, sir, I think that first we will see a small black dot far away on the horizon. As we get closer, the black dot will become as big as an upside-down teacup. As we get still closer, it will look like an inverted soup bowl. Finally, we should be able to make out the ridges of that island."

Mr. Hoshino was perceptive in his thoughts, but his conclusion was based on our still having our eyesight. Nothing would be more tragic than not being able to recognize land, even though it was there. I prayed eagerly that we would reach shore before losing our eyesight.

On this day the senior officer passed the word to the staff officers to develop an action plan against enemy submarines, for we were approaching the area where they might be expected.

We decided that if we were fired upon by an enemy submarine, we would fire back with the machine gun. Otherwise we would not make an attack upon her.

We expected that the enemy would come over to our boats to capture several officers to collect information; we would not resist and some officers would board the submarine. After boarding I would get close to the enemy captain, standing next to him, and then other officers would step between the captain and his men to block their access to him. At the right moment I would take the captain as a hostage with my concealed short sword and intimidate him into towing our boats to the Philippines.

Based on our plan, the senior officer updated the men at the boat officers' assembly saying:

"I believe there are a good number of enemy submarines in the waters off the Philippines. Our antisubmarine action plan is this: We will not make an attack upon them, as our machine gun will not be effective against a submarine. However, if we are fired upon, we will shoot back, aiming at the officers on the bridge, and not at the hull. The enemy will probably come over to our boats to capture some officers to get information. In that case, I want you to be quiet and not to move. When the enemy takes some of us to their sub, the communications officer will go with them, and choose the right time to intimidate the enemy captain with his concealed short sword and take over the sub. After he has done this, we will have control over them."

I noticed that many of the men did not think our plan to sea-jack a submarine could possibly be carried out. Then someone shouted, "If we take over an enemy sub, we will be treated to Roosevelt rations, and you can eat all you want. It's much better than being half dead!"

I was glad that there was one person who tried to boost the morale of the crew, though we all knew that a machine gun and a short sword are ineffective weapons against the enemy.

In the glow of the sunset that evening I reminisced about a crimson sunset in Manchuria.

In August 1940, we made a port of call at Talien harbor in Manchuria aboard a training squadron for newly commissioned ensigns. At a reception, the president of the South Manchurian Railway gave us an address. "We had a request from the Training Squadron Headquarters to arrange second-class coaches for your trip to Changchun. Because you will be serving in the navy, I do not suppose you will ever return to Manchuria. Therefore, I have decided to arrange first-class coaches for you. This is my treat. I hope you enjoy your trip to Manchuria. Thank you."

Thanks to his kindness, I really enjoyed watching the crimson setting sun from a first-class coach on the world-famous train, The Asia, of the South Manchurian Railway.

In those days Japan was enjoying great prosperity, and Germany, with whom Japan had entered into an alliance, was sweeping over the whole of Europe and still gathering momentum. I was young and quite optimistic about visiting Manchuria many times in the future.

Only four years had elapsed since then. But about half of my

288 classmates had already died in action. For many, that trip to Manchuria had become their last, as the president had said. Although I was still alive, I was in a boat, drifting in the vast Pacific Ocean. I was not sure if I would ever return to Japan, much less to visit Manchuria.

I feared I was getting too sentimental, which would make me ineffective as a naval officer, so I turned away my gaze of the setting sun.

31

August 28
Bearing Death Always
in My Thoughts

At this point I thought about those who had died on our boats. The first died from fatigue soon after he was taken aboard. Then five died who had suffered burns in the explosion after the torpedo hit on our ship. Over fifty percent of their bodies were burned, and we had no way to treat them. Those who died next were four men who swam until they were completely exhausted, and never recovered from their fatigue.

The senior officer asked me on this day what I had in mind as a last resort, in case we concluded that we could not reach shore.

I replied that I was thinking of writing about the *Natori* boat unit on a thin piece of cloth with blood obtained by cutting my finger, putting in into a cider bottle, and throwing it into the sea. But he objected to my idea, saying, "Your idea isn't practical, Mr. Matsunaga, for there is no thin piece of cloth in our boat. For my part, I was thinking of engraving this message on the stern sheets or a thwart with a sharp object obtained by taking the machine gun apart. `August date, 1944. HIJMS *Natori* boat unit. Three boats. Navigator Lt. Eiichi Kobayashi and 184 others.' Of the three boats, at least one may drift with the North Pacific Current and reach a place occupied by Japanese forces. However, don't let anyone notice what we're talking about."

For the past ten days, I had carefully avoided speaking words such as the last moment and death. But now, some men had already died from fatigue, and the other men's exhaustion had also become so conspicuous that even the senior officer could no longer avoid considering death.

At the boat officers' assembly, though, the senior officer did not give any indication that he was considering the crew's death. I cried out in my mind:

"God, up to now, we have made our efforts, bit by bit, without praying for divine aid. But I suspect that within a few days we will reach the limit of our physical strength. We need some evidence that we are close to land. God, please give us a change within a day or two. Please."

Mr. Yamashita, who had been on duty as boat officer, came up to me and whispered into my ear. "Mr. Matsunaga, Petty Officer Kojima, now rowing the fifth position, is in pretty bad shape. I told him to take a rest tonight, but he wouldn't listen to me. He said he would be letting down the other men if he took a rest. I'll take his place when my duty is over."

"Good thinking, Number Nine. If someone else is in bad shape, I will take over his position."

Although I thought about death from time to time, I tried to follow the senior officer's lead, for he deliberately ignored death as he struggled to accomplish his mission. But because he brought it up, I thought I should consider my own death.

The counsel of one of my teachers in my high school days to "study hard and set your goal to serve the country" gave me courage to leave my hometown for a naval career. With the war going on, I had very few opportunities to return for a visit. Now I was in a boat drifting in the Pacific Ocean, and I wondered whether I would ever reach shore. Oddly enough, I pined very much for my hometown.

My grandmother had brought me up from the time I was five years old, in the small rural village of Rokuda. To rear me as a strong healthy boy, she would never let me eat frozen treats or shaved ice, for she believed a child would not grow healthy if his stomach had been chilled. She claimed she would not buy such things for me because she was careful with her money, but then she would buy me bananas instead, which were more expensive than a bowl of shaved ice. Once a month she would prepare miso soup with chopped leek in it to exterminate round worms.

She had peculiar treatments for me when I was sick. Whenever I had a cold, she would prepare a bowl of steaming hot noodles for me, and put me to bed with a foot warmer. She said, "It is better to stay in bed than to see a doctor or take medicine." When I had diarrhea, she would make me skip one meal, so that I could recover with my own strength, and not depend on a doctor or some medicine. Because of my grandmother's care, I grew up stronger and healthier than others.

The last time I saw her was in February 1941, when my ship was anchored at Sasebo Naval Base, and I took a three-hour train ride to surprise her in Rokuta. I was her first-born grandson, whom she had raised with loving care, and she was overjoyed. But unfortunately, the excitement of my visit was too much for her, and she became very ill. The doctor said that she had a stroke and needed complete rest.

Because I was in training as a junior officer, I could not get leave to care for her, so I asked the neighbors to care for my grandmother, and returned to my ship. After completing scheduled fleet maneuvers we returned to our home port, where a letter from my mother was awaiting me. I learned that grandmother had died shortly after she had been taken ill. Soon after this, the war with the United States began, and since that time I had been serving at the front line, and had not been able to do my homage to grandmother's grave.

As I reflected on this, I muttered to myself, "Grandma, I have had my ship sunk three times, and I have often been in danger. But here I am, without a scratch. Perhaps you have saved my life. Now I am in a boat drifting in the Pacific Ocean. Remember you taught me, 'No need to fear thunderclaps in the direction of *tatsu mi*, for they only roar.' That came in handy, Grandma. If I ever return home, I will surely pay a visit to your grave."

I had been at the front since the outbreak of the war, but came home after my ship had sunk in a battle and saw my mother in Tokyo. During this visit, she always wanted to take me out to watch a *kabuki* play or the grand *sumo* wrestling. Apparently, because there was no knowing when I might die in action, she wanted to show me these great performances I had never seen and were available only in Tokyo.

Although I understood her intentions, I had my own opinion. A legend says you will return when you have something on your heart. I thought that if I did not watch these performances now, I would live to return home and watch them, so I did not go to the performances. She also prepared special treats, including *zenzai* and *shiruko* (sweet red bean soup with rice cakes). But since I had already

163

acquired a taste for sake, I no longer cared for sweets, and I also declined these.

Thinking over how I treated her until now, I realized that my actions had made her sad and worried. I decided that if I ever returned to my homeland, I would go to the these performances, and eat the sweets she prepared.

32

August 28
Commanding Officer's Insight

On this day, August 28, we saw no land, and that night we were forced to row against the wind. Stocker Petty Officer Koura, a member of the fishing squad, addressed me.

"Sir, when I was a fisherman before joining the navy, I learned that man's power is helpless against Nature. Therefore, fishermen never row into the wind, and I don't think we should either."

No one could blame him for his remarks. We had been rowing and rowing for almost ten days, and still had not seen any indication that we were near land. And unless Petty Officer Koura saw some specific objects related to land, it would be hard for him to listen to me. I was not sure how to respond when Yeoman First Class Yamamoto, of the same fishing squad, stood up and challenged the crew.

"We have to admit there is an element of truth in what Petty Officer Koura said. We have rowed for the past ten days, placing our confidence in the senior officer's decisions. We must be nearing land, even though we have not seen it yet. Suppose we would quit rowing right here, where only one more major push is needed. Then, all our efforts up to now would go down the drain, wouldn't they? Let's keep rowing for a couple more days or so."

Shouts of "That's right" and "Let's do that" rose here and there in the boat, and the consensus was to keep rowing. At the same time, I recognized that there was a dissenting voice. I was relieved that so far we had avoided a mutiny, but I wondered how many more days the men would have sufficient strength to continue rowing.

For the ship's biscuits to last thirty days, each person was rationed one three-gram biscuit twice each day. As there were twenty biscuits packed in each waxed paper bag, twenty men shared a bag at each meal. This paper bag also contained two tiny sugarplums, and because we could not divide these among twenty men, I collected them. After a rainsquall had continued for a length of time, or when we were all done in, I dissolved these sugarplums in water using a canteen, and passed it among the men. It was a welcome change in our monotonous life in the boat, and gave us much encouragement.

The senior officer referred to this at the boat officers' assembly. "I really appreciated the sugar water. Come to think of it, we also owe this to Captain Kubota, for just before our ship went down, he instructed me to take the ship's biscuits and water canteens along. We should never forget his kindness."

Then the senior officer gave a very significant order. "We will reach the Philippines within a day or two. I want ten persons to be selected out of each boat to serve on a coconut-gathering detail. Choose those who are strong, healthy, and neatly dressed, and if possible, good athletes. Take a machine gun. Mr. Matsunaga, you take charge of the party."

It was difficult to identify those who were not only healthy but also neatly dressed and agile. Then I observed some heartwarming sights. Those who were still neatly dressed were offering their uniforms to those who were healthy and athletic. Some men voluntarily offered their tennis shoes as well.

There were many things to consider in organizing this detail. It would be essential to proceed slowly and carefully to the beach so that we would not ruin the boat on any underwater obstructions. Further, we could not assume that the residents would be friendly, so there was the possibility of the boat being damaged by rifle fire. We should not carry out our plan at night because our night vision was severely limited by the lack of food and the strain we had experienced.

Coco palms with coconuts at the top of the trunks grow near the coastline everywhere in the tropics. Each palm bears about twenty coconuts four times each year. The coconut milk has a sugary taste, although it smells somewhat grassy, and would quench our thirst. When cracked open, there is a layer of edible white copra, which is sweet and delicious. But the trunk of the coco palms stands upright, about sixty feet high and ten inches in diameter, with no branches. It's hard enough for a healthy man to climb to its top, much less for one of the men in our outfit, so gathering coconuts in this way was out of the question. And if we tried to steal coconuts from the natives, the guerillas would most likely attack us. The same would be true if we took bananas or papayas, which were planted near the natives' houses.

I decided that I would have to clarify what the senior officer had in mind before setting out for the shore. At any rate, I suspected that he had passed the word about organizing a coconut-gathering party as food for thought and to build up the men's hopes. I certainly admired his talent in thinking of various topics, one after another, such as antisubmarine actions and organizing a coconut-gathering party.

The days that followed the *Hardhead*'s return to its assigned area were relatively uneventful. Some were spent submerged as we patrolled close to shore. In this case the OOD was the key person, for he manned the periscope and was truly the "eyes" of the boat, and was backed up by the crew member who manned the sound gear, the "ears" of the boat.

On other days we patrolled on the surface, farther from shore, though usually still within sight of land. In this operation five lookouts and the OOD were on the bridge, keeping a sharp lookout for enemy planes as well as searching for ships. Almost every day that we patrolled on the surface we had at least one plane contact, either visually or on radar, at which time we would dive immediately.

When we left port we had taken ten movies, most relatively old, with us, and on some of these uneventful days we showed a movie in the forward torpedo room. The first showing was about 1800, and the second about 2015, to accommodate those who came off watch at 2000. It was a unique sight to see men viewing a movie on a screen in front of the torpedo tubes, with the beam of the projector reflecting off the torpedoes on either side, and crew members trying to get comfortable on various cushions on the steel deck. When a movie started while we were submerged, the diving officer had to adjust the amount of water in the ballast tanks to compensate for the weight of the additional men in the forward part of the boat.

The morning of August 28 stands out in my mind, for as I was serving as OOD at daybreak I sighted a ship through my binoculars. It was a startling experience, for after keeping a sharp lookout for many days and sighting nothing, I could scarcely believe my eyes when it occurred. This was the first time, apart from the ship we sank, that we sighted an enemy ship. I asked the lookout responsible for that sector of the horizon if he saw a ship, and he confirmed the sighting. I immediately called the captain to the bridge, and began coaching the radar operator onto the target, who ascertained the range to be 10,000 yards.

Because the target was headed toward us and it was already getting light, we had no choice but to dive, which we did two minutes after sighting the ship. We began a submerged approach, and determined that the ship was a destroyer traveling at high speed and zigging radically. We could not get close enough to attack, and regretfully broke off the approach. This encounter reminded us that Surigao Strait did have some ship movement through it.

33

August 28
Has the Senior Officer Gone Mad?

"An island, right twenty degrees. Distance unknown!" a look-out shouted in excitement. For the past few days, I had received a similar report shortly after 1000, and then another report about 1600 stating that the island disappeared. The lookouts took turns each day, which meant that different lookouts repeatedly made the same report.

I began to check these observations myself. Sure enough, I found the dark islandlike object lying far away, not moving a bit as I watched it for more than an hour. No one could blame a seaman who saw a stationary dark object on the horizon and took it for an island. Then, around 1600, as the sun declined westward and began shining on the islandlike object from behind, it would scatter and vanish in a moment. Each day we were very much discouraged when the island vanished.

This day, as I was lying down on the bottom of our boat, I decided to pay no attention to the lookout's report of sighting an island. Though I was not asleep, I kept my eyes closed as I tried to charge my battery for the coming night. Then I felt someone shaking me as he called, "Mr. Matsunaga, Mr. Matsunaga." I lazily opened my eyes and found it was Petty Officer Ishikawa.

"Mr. Matsunaga, the island is the real thing today, sir."

As he spoke he looked into my face with an earnestness I

could not ignore. So I rose up and looked, but to me it was no different from what we had seen on previous days. I then noticed the senior officer looking at me, signaling with his eyes. Yet, seeing the serious look on Petty Officer Ishikawa's face, I could not turn him away in ridicule or anger.

"Ishikawa, the way I look at it, it hasn't changed a bit since yesterday. It's not an island."

"Sir, I've been watching it for over two hours. It hasn't moved a bit. It's a real island, all right, sir. If we began rowing now, we would be there before sundown. We have been rowing every day without having decent meals, and we can't do this forever. Mr. Matsunaga, let's get going now, and get to that island before the day is over."

"Ishikawa, listen to me carefully. I want you to remember we are following a deliberate plan, and according to the plan, we take a break in the daytime. It is not a rest for the sake of rest, but to prepare for ten hours of rowing at night. In our conversation with the senior officer last night, he did not give us permission to row toward an islandlike object if we sighted one. We will not row toward that island today."

Petty Officer Ishikawa unwillingly consented to my words. But no one could blame him for his determination and enthusiasm, because his suggestion was based on his serious concern about how much longer our physical strength would hold up.

I disliked being disturbed and having a discussion about a nonexisting island in the daytime when I should have been sleeping, but at least there was a redeeming feature or saving grace on this day. A few days ago, I had passed the word to Mr. Yamashita and Mr. Hoshino not to talk directly to the senior officer. My thinking must have rubbed off among the men. Wasn't that why Petty Officer Ishikawa talked to me, the second in command, instead of talking directly to the senior officer? If so, I was glad from the standpoint of maintaining military discipline in our extreme circumstances.

Having made this decision, I was dozing off again when it suddenly became noisy around me, and I heard someone speak out in a high-pitched tone, "A butterfly!" Though I had my doubts, I rose to look for myself and saw a little white butterfly flying only two meters from us. It looked very much like those I used to chase when I was a boy. Although I was usually an impious person, I really thought it a heaven-sent gift for us, and was grateful to God for giving the men another topic to talk about. Also, I concluded that the butterfly could at the most fly only five to ten miles out to sea from the coast. If that was true, perhaps we could reach shore if we rowed for three or four hours. Everyone was lighthearted and grinning.

"Mr. Matsunaga, let's get going. What are we waiting for?"

Encouraging shouts arose here and there. I realized that this was not the sentiment of a few men, but the will of the entire crew.

"Okay, you guys, we'll get going. All hands, get up!"

So urging the men, I then reported, without formality, to the senior officer. "Senior Officer, we'll begin rowing now, sir."

All hands rowed each stroke with their whole heart and all their might. We were in such high spirits that we forgot all about our fatigue and the terrible heat. The boat moved swiftly on and on, making us wonder how in the world we, who had not had enough food, water, and rest for ten days, had such latent physical strength.

"O–n–e, t–w–o." With a spare tiller, I encouraged the oarsmen by keeping time with their strokes like we used to do during the long–range boat race at the Naval Academy. Oarsmen could not see the object to which the boat was proceeding, for their backs were facing it. But on this day, they bent to the oars and did not seem to be worrying about where the boat was headed. As the sun began to set in the west, the enchanted 1600 hour neared. Alas! As it had on the previous days, the islandlike object completely dissipated like mist.

"Easy all. Rest on your oars. Take them in. Break."

Everyone turned around and was taken aback. It was incredible to find that the islandlike object, which should have been there, was gone and nowhere to be seen! We all fell down, like decayed old trees, and did not utter a word. Our disappointment was far worse than our physical fatigue.

It was too late to cry over spilt milk. I lay down like the others, and soon was sound asleep. I was still tired and sleepy when I felt someone repeatedly shaking me out of my sleep, saying the senior officer wanted me. As I sat up very lazily, he yelled out orders at me.

"Mr. Matsunaga, what are you waiting for? It's about time to begin rowing! Get going right away!"

Only half awake, I did not understand what he was yelling. When I did not get moving, he shouted at me again, demanding I take immediate action.

Until a few days ago, there were no disagreements between the senior officer and me about our thinking. However, over the past few days, as we considered the details of coming ashore, I had to admit that our thoughts diverged, and I sensed a rift between us. For the sake of accomplishing our vital mission, I suppressed my feelings as much as I could, but I could not take it anymore and talked back to him.

"Senior officer, look, everyone is asleep because they are dead tired. Please let them sleep just one night. I plead for a break. We have already covered the planned distance for the day."

"I don't give a damn what you did in the daytime, Mr. Matsunaga. I did not pass the word to row, but you did that of your own accord. Remember? We are now in combat action. Rowing for ten hours by night is the scheduled action. Get to work according to the plan, bear a hand! Did you hear?"

"Aye aye, sir. We will get going right away."

"Hey, wake up, you guys. We must get moving to the Philippines. Get your behinds on the thwarts!"

"Prepare oars. Ready, give way. . . ."

All hands began rowing without a syllable of complaint. The boat did not move as swiftly as it had in the daytime, yet their oars-manship was orderly and left nothing to be desired. If they had been rowing against their will, they could not have kept strokes as harmoniously. They were obviously trained military personnel, and survivors of the *Natori.*

Seeing the men rowing in dead silence, I shouted in my mind, "If I were the senior officer, you wouldn't be chained to oars like this. I would let you have a good night's sleep. I asked him nicely to let you have rest just for tonight. Then what happened? As you all know, he turned me down flat. If I had protested one more word, he could have accused me of being insubordinate. Insubordination before an enemy could result in a sentence of death. You have to understand my position."

The senior officer's attitude just did not fit right today. Why did he, who had always been so considerate of his subordinates, now make a completely unreasonable demand of us? When I reported to him that we were going to row in the daytime, he could have turned me down right on the spot if he had not wanted us to row. He was conniving, allowing us to row for five hours by day, and then demanding that we row another ten hours by night. I truly felt like he had cheated us.

He had always told his staff officers, as though it were his pet phrase, "Don't ever play cheap tricks on your men. If you do, they will not place their confidence in you. Should this happen, we will never be able to accomplish our mission."

The senior officer played a cheap trick this night, and this made my blood boil, for what he had stubbornly done to us was contrary to his fine preaching.

I had a hunch they might mutiny this night. I secretly whispered into Mr. Yamashita's ear.

"Hi, Number Nine. I'm afraid they might rebel against the senior officer tonight. When I'm off, I will mingle with the oarsmen and row. I want you to do the same when you're off."

I could understand why the senior officer, as commanding officer of the outfit, became irritated under the circumstances. But at the same time, it should be his duty to restrain himself when feeling impatient, shouldn't it?

The senior officer who had always been very considerate of his men, suddenly became so stubborn that we were nearly chained to the oars. Has he gone mad?

PART EIGHT

RETURNED ALIVE

34

August 29
The Ridges of an Island

The day dawned and it was August 29. On the previous day we had rowed for five hours in the daytime and ended up rowing for another ten hours at night. When the scheduled night action was over about 0400, all hands were so physically and mentally exhausted that they lay down as though they were dead. Then, in the morning twilight, I heard someone shout.

"Look, a palm leaf. There it is!"

A floating object from land had finally appeared. Although I was very tired, I stood up to look. Sure enough, it was a palm leaf. To our eyes, which had seen nothing but navy blue waters for over ten days, its green color was beautifully bright and fresh. I looked at that featureless palm leaf with gratitude, as though it were a servant sent by God.

When we saw the butterfly on the previous day, we were in seventh heaven with joy, for land was not far away. But when I thought it over more carefully, I realized that a butterfly could have been carried far out to sea by the wind. Compared with that butterfly, the floating palm leaf was a much stronger indication that we were near land.

Although everyone was tired out, I hoped that seeing the palm leaf this morning would encourage them for at least one more day.

"Oh, I see something dark over there!" someone suddenly

shouted with awe. As I peered through the pale light, I also sighted something dark lying on the horizon, far to the left.

When we were drifting in the sea after the disaster, we had no idea that we could reach shore by ourselves. Our only hope was to be rescued. But now, after rowing with all our might for more than ten days, and encountering some promising indications that land was near, we had reached the point where we hoped we could go ashore without anyone else's help.

We were also cautious about going ashore, however, for we were well aware of the danger of confronting guerillas. Even though we had struggled alone for ten days, we wanted, if at all possible, to go ashore without encountering anyone.

As for the dark object on the horizon, we would have to wait for the first gray of dawn to determine what it was. We had been deceived by the word "land" often enough to make a saint swear, and this time we wanted to be sure before we congratulated ourselves on sighting land.

We found that the dark object was unmistakably an island. Much to my surprise, we were looking at the ridges of the island. What we, the staff officers, had expected to see when nearing land was, first of all, a dark dot far away, which would grow to be like an inverted teacup, and then look like a soup bowl. Only later did we expect to see the ridges of the island. In reality, a clearly visible island had suddenly made its appearance.

Before I could find my bearings in the circumstance, I was astonished to hear the senior officer murmur, "That's Hinatuan Passage." As navigator, he had checked the topography of that area whenever the *Natori* passed there, and he recognized it as Hinatuan Passage from the shape of the surrounding ridges.

If we were at Hinatuan Passage, our boat unit, which had been headed for Samar Island, had drifted a few hundred miles to the south. I then thought more about the tide in the area and why we had drifted so far south.

During our voyage I was very much concerned about the ocean current, and I paid no attention to the tide. An ocean current corresponds to a river in the ocean, which flows at a given place in a definite direction. In these waters, we were in the North Equatorial Current (known as the Japan Current when passing off the coast of Japan), which flows from east to west.

Tide is the phenomenon by which the surface of the sea alternately rises and falls twice a day, caused by the attraction of the moon and the sun. Near rivers and straits there is a horizontal movement of the seawater associated with the tides called a tidal current. The direction of flow of a tidal current is reversed when the flood tide changes to an ebb tide.

Because the Philippines consists of many islands, large and small, many straits or channels are open to the Pacific Ocean. As a seaman, I should have realized that as we neared shore there would be tidal currents. But I was so preoccupied with the ocean current that I forgot all about the tidal currents at these straits or channels.

Then I realized what had happened on the day before. Seeing the butterfly in the morning, we began rowing. At the beginning, the boats were moving at a great speed. However, even though we kept rowing with all our might, we did not seem to make much progress.

That night, when the senior officer forced us to row, we came within sight of the ridges of the island despite our reluctance. From this, I concluded that in the afternoon, despite our efforts, the boats did not go far because of the adverse tidal current. But with the favorable tidal current at night, we covered a great distance.

Because we did not have a tide table, the senior officer could not possibly have known when the tide would turn. Instead he must have concluded that we had reached our physical limit and decided we could not afford to waste any more time. At any rate, because of the senior officer's determination we reached land that morning. This reminded me of what Lt. Comdr. Rikihei Inoguchi, the instructor in the science of command and leadership, told us at the Naval Academy:

"Because you have no experience in taking charge of actual sailors, you must take it for granted that an ideal commanding officer is one who has an excellent understanding of all factors relating to ships and the sea, and is also a gracious man of good sense. But he must be heartless and obstinate in certain situations." The senior officer had certainly been a very strict disciplinarian the night before!

To this point we had set up a mast to sail every day. On this day, however, we did not set up a mast, fearing that it might be sighted by guerillas on the land. Because we had rowed for fifteen hours on the previous day, we decided to take a good rest all day long. All three boats gathered close together, let out sea anchors, and drifted. Although the sea was not raging, we hoped the sea anchors would prevent us from being pushed off shore by the tidal current.

Seaman First Class Ishimura of the second department, in the leading boat, and Petty Officer Second Class Takahashi, in the third boat, died on this day, and we quietly buried them at sea after sunset. They had both been so exhausted on the rafts that they did not recover from fatigue. Takahashi was in such bad shape when he was pulled out of the water into the boat that he was talking in delirium, saying, "I'm transferred to the Shanghai landing party, and am on my way there, sir." Later the third-boat officer told me that Petty Officer Kobayashi had been looking after him with tenderest care, taking off his jacket and putting it on Takahashi. It was certainly pathetic that they died in action so close to land. If only they had made it ashore, we could have given them much better care.

I was also informed that Seaman First Class Yamada had swallowed heavy oil while in the sea, and had been in bad shape. Would he be all right until we came ashore?

35

August 29
Restraining Ourselves from
Proceeding to the Shore

On this day, at the boat officers' assembly, the senior officer passed this word: "As you all know, we have had very little nourishment for the past ten days, and everyone is night–blinded. Therefore, we must avoid getting close to the shore in the evening. If we begin rowing as usual immediately after sundown, we would reach shore during the night, and we could not see if we encountered guerillas.

"I know very well that everyone wants to hit the beach as soon as possible. But remember, we must put the finishing touch on whatever we do. It's been said of old, 'There's many a slip twixt the cup and the lip.' We must be extra cautious under these circumstances. When the time is right I will pass the word about when we will proceed to the shore."

It was difficult to restrain ourselves from setting out right away and we heard a voice here and there urging that we proceed to the shore. But the senior officer remained adamant.

It was late at night when the senior officer finally passed the word to begin rowing. In the sky, I saw that Cassiopeia had already rotated sixty degrees from where it had been at sunset, which meant it was almost midnight.

During the early stage of our voyage, the senior officer and his staff were unanimous about what should be done, but as we neared

181

land, the senior officer's attitude was far more prudent than his staff's.

I recalled that when we began our long voyage, Mr. Yamashita predicted that the noctilucae would be more evident as we got close to shore. He was right, for the noctilucae were now extremely luminous, and an almost full moon was too bright for us, for we would be clearly visible to guerillas.

"Moon, would you please not shine so brightly? Noctilucae would you not be so luminous?" I thought. For the past ten days or so, we kept rowing toward an invisible goal, using our best judgment to give us direction. But not this night. There was an island. Yes, there it was, right in front of us! We unconsciously threw our energy into the oars. Some men were grinning as they worked diligently at rowing.

About thirty minutes after we set out with great hope, we heard "dah, dah, dah"—the sound of engines. We were petrified and the joyful atmosphere that prevailed in the boats vanished in a moment. It sounded like the diesel engines of a submarine. I then immediately passed the word.

"Prepare for antisubmarine battle. Execute!" Each boat simultaneously untied the painter, as we had planned. The leading boat continued to proceed dead ahead, the second boat deploying to the right, and the third boat to the left. All three boats began charging at the submarine, when the senior officer said, "Mr. Matsunaga, listen. The detonation does not sound like diesel engines. It sounds more like a hot-bulb engine."

I was very tense and all ears.

"Pon, pon, pon." Sure enough, the sound was the p-sound, which meant a hot-bulb engine. This meant that the ship had to be friendly.

"Knock off antisubmarine battle. Stow the gear. Easy all. Take 'em in."

"All hands, shout out, lend a hand!"

Look! The ship changed its course to proceed away from us. Realizing how tragic this would be, we all yelled as though for our very lives. And then it happened. The ship made a 180_ turn, and returned toward us. What a great sigh of relief we all gave! As we were told later on, those on the ship saw three white-crested waves suddenly rise right in front of them, and thought they would be attacked by enemy PT boats. But when they heard us call in Japanese, they quickly responded.

This hot-bulb engine vessel was transporting shifts of soldiers to army observation posts. After some discussion and negotiation, they agreed to tow our three boats to Surigao, a town on the northeastern part of Mindanao Island.

Because the crew of this army vessel had little experience in towing other vessels, the senior officer and I transferred to this vessel to assist. The senior officer moved into position beside the skipper of this army vessel, and I stationed myself on the stern above the propeller. The skipper prudently repeated forward and stop engine orders, and the ship gradually picked up speed, during which time, I lifted the towline from the water with a boat hook so that it would not become entangled in the propeller.

Finally, we were in towing condition. Judging from the white waves at the bow, I estimated the vessel was making at least six knots. As we had proceeded at three knots throughout our voyage, the vessel's speed really made our heads spin.

Suddenly we spotted a signal flare being shot up from shore into the dark sky. According to a crew member of the army vessel, they had often seen these signal flares while making scheduled runs along the coast, and concluded that guerillas were using them to communicate with enemy submarines offshore. This was most disconcerting, for having reached shore after undergoing hardships beyond description, the thought of now being killed was more than we could bear. We prayed earnestly that the army vessel would enter the mouth of Hinatuan Passage as soon as possible.

I must admit that human beings are certainly inconsistent creatures. When the towing operation began, we thought it was great that the army vessel was making six knots. But once we were exposed to the danger of being killed by the enemy, we were quickly impatient with that speed.

At long last, we passed the mouth of the passage. As I realized we had finally reached a safe zone, I felt very thirsty. From my knowledge of ships, I guessed the location of a water tank in this vessel. Thinking that only God knew, I lifted the cover of the tank, scooped some water with a dipper, and drank it.

"Matsunaga! Have you forgotten the precept `senyu koraku'? [This phrase means to always be alert before your subordinates, and have your enjoyment or pleasure after them, and was used to explain one of the techniques of command/leadership.] Aren't you ashamed of yourself, as a regular officer? Are you worthy of being in command?"

The nearby army soldiers were flabbergasted as the senior officer suddenly thundered against his second in command. I knew there was no excuse whatsoever for what I had done, and I drooped my head in shame.

The senior officer, on the other hand, was truly a man of noble character. Not until he ascertained that all hands had water, after going ashore the following morning, did he have his share. This reminded me once again that it was because of the senior officer's sublime character that the men did not mutiny during the voyage, even when they were forced to undergo almost unbearable hardships.

I saw some soldiers in the army vessel busily cooking, and thought they were preparing their midnight meal. Soon afterward, a soldier offered a bowl of rice gruel to the senior officer and me. The senior officer expressed his hearty gratitude to the skipper, but said he wanted to have the crew in the boats eat first. We then sent the bowls to the boats by using the towlines.

Because we were 183 freeloaders on a vessel with a ten-man crew, the rice gruel they shared did not amount to much for each person; although it was a trifle, the crew of the boat unit would never forget, throughout their lives, the wonderful taste of the rice gruel they had on this night.

36

August 30
The Painters Were Untied

Soon the first signs of light appeared in the eastern sky and the stars began to disappear. This was August 30, twelve days after we watched with horror and dismay as the *Natori* slipped below the surface.

For the past twelve days we had seen nothing but blue, and had experienced withering cold and scorching heat. But that morning we saw green all around us, and looked forward to being a part of human society again.

The thought of soon going ashore put us in very high spirits and the animated conversation of the men in the boats drifted to the army vessel.

The senior officer, watching the boat unit near the quay, passed the following word to me: "Mr. Matsunaga, semaphore this message to each boat. 'We will soon untie the painters and approach the quay. All hands tidy yourselves up and maintain strict military discipline, and thereby bring this voyage to a successful conclusion.'"

Each boat acknowledged receipt of the semaphore, and in each I saw the men sitting face to face as they helped one another tidy up. Considering the shortage of water and food they had undergone for many days, their movement was energetic and snappy, which convinced me that they would make good landings at the quay.

Three rising suns, the naval ensigns, were fluttering in the wind conspicuously and triumphantly.

"Mr. Matsunaga, semaphore to each boat, 'The *Natori* boat unit dismissed. Each boat proceed to the quay and moor alongside. Untie the painters.'" The painters were untied, and each boat proceeded to its destination, the quay.

The army vessel tied up briefly at the quay, and after expressing hearty thanks to its crew, the senior officer and I landed. As we had not walked for the past twelve days, we felt our knees knock as we staggered along.

We admitted that, under the circumstances, the plans we had made for seajacking a submarine or gathering coconuts were as significant as wax fruit, and laughed at ourselves. As we talked, we watched each boat as they made beautiful landings, and it was as though heavy loads were lifted from our shoulders.

Chief Petty Officer Watanabe, one of the members of the fishing squad, walked up to the senior officer and said, "I beg your pardon, Senior Officer, for having made an indiscreet remark at the scene of the disaster, sir. It is entirely through your wise and prudent decisions that we are back on shore again. I truly thank you, Senior Officer, sir."

"Watanabe, before our departure for the long voyage, we had a discussion that made us determined to overcome fate and accomplish the voyage, no matter how difficult it might be. We owe our success to all hands, for they did their very best in harmony."

"With you, sir, I would go anywhere, even to Hawaii. I really mean it."

Through his brief words, I realized his great trust in, and gratitude to, the senior officer.

The boats were moored alongside the quay, and the oars, in use for the past twelve days, were stowed away in the boats. As the men realized that their lives were no longer in danger, the strain that had appeared on their faces was rapidly disappearing.

Because the men had not walked for twelve days, and were now somewhat relaxed, some found it difficult to climb by themselves out of the boats, but the army soldiers were kind enough to give them a helping hand. Most of them staggered as they walked to their billets, and a few sailors were leaning on the shoulders of the army soldiers as they walked. Seeing this, Petty Officer Yamamoto shouted out, "What's the matter with you guys, leaning against someone else's shoulders? Act like sailors! Shape up and walk with your own feet!"

Suddenly they were brought to their senses. Until then, we were pretending to ourselves that doing this might be permissible, because we had undergone such indescribable hardships. But by Petty Officer Yamamoto's thunder, that babyish notion was completely blown away.

I was watching the boats and the men at the quay, when an unfamiliar naval officer came up and spoke to me.

"I'm Surgeon Lieutenant (jg) Togawa, the officer in charge of the 31st PT boat unit, sir. I had a dispatch from the Army Headquarters here that a naval boat unit would be arriving at the quay, and so I've come to meet with you. Our outfit consists of twenty personnel including myself, and no other naval unit is stationed in this town. If there is anything we can do for you, please do not hesitate to ask us. We will be happy to do whatever we can," he said.

"By the way," he added, "is there a medical corps officer in your outfit, sir? If not, please designate me your medical corps officer."

I was deeply impressed with his proposal, for he took the trouble to come all the way to the quay to meet with us, and voluntarily offered medical care. After talking with the senior officer, we decided to accept his kind proposal because we needed his medical treatment.

As the Togawa unit had no radio communication equipment, I needed to visit the Army Headquarters about two kilometers from the quay by bicycle. I tried to ride the bicycle and fell down with a thud because my body was so stiff that I could not stretch out my arms and legs sufficiently. Many people nearby urged me to give up trying, saying it was too risky, but I tried again, and once the bicycle started moving it was quite easy. The five years I rode my bicycle to high school were quite helpful to me now.

The Army Headquarters was on the top of a slightly elevated plateau. Mr. Togawa had already notified them of my visit by telephone, so I was immediately ushered into the office of the staff officer, Lt. Col. Tomoichi Hidaka.

"I am naval Lieutenant Matsunaga, sir. Our *Natori* boat unit, consisting of three boats, encountered an army vessel at Hinatuan Passage last night, and we were towed to Surigao and landed here. Our senior officer, Lieutenant Kobayashi, is now taking charge of getting the billets ready for the night. As the second in command, I came here on his behalf to thank you, sir."

"We appreciate your coming all the way to visit us after your long arduous voyage," he said, thanking me for my trouble. "If there is anything we can do to help you, please do not hesitate to ask us."

"Thank you very much, sir. First of all, I would like to have a status report on our outfit dispatched to our Fleet Headquarters in Manila. Second, we'd like to ask for a loan of clothing, blankets, and two-week provisions for 185 officers and men. These items will be returned to you by the navy at a later date, sir."

"We'll be happy to send this communication and see to it that you will have these items. Incidentally, Lieutenant Matsunaga, if you don't mind, would you please tell us about your boat unit and the voyage, to the extent you are permitted, if that wouldn't be too inconvenient?" he said, offering me a chair.

"Although there is no chain of command between us, I will keep standing and report the situation to you," I said. "Please excuse me keeping my feet apart, as I cannot stand at attention."

With this introduction, I told the following story in front of about ten army staff officers.

"Since June of this year, the *Natori* had been engaged in the transport of urgently required supplies from Manila to Palau. On our fourth trip to Palau, the *Natori* was torpedoed by an enemy submarine and went down, about three hundred miles east of Samar Island, a distance equivalent to that between Tokyo and Osaka. Our commanding officer, Captain Kubota, met his fate with his ship. Of the six hundred ship's company, two hundred officers and men were left behind in three boats, in the vast ocean. A medium-attack bomber flew over us, spotting the boats, and dropped a message cylinder, promising the arrival of rescue ships. But the senior officer figured that the possibility of being sighted by the rescue ships was so slim that he decided we should proceed to the Philippines on our own, against everyone else's opposition. We sailed by day and rowed for ten hours by night. Having no compass or chronometer, we determined the direction to the west by observing the stars at night. We lived on two ship's biscuits a day, and drank water from rainsqualls."

After a few questions, Lt. Col. Hidaka concluded the meeting by saying, "I suppose you have undergone hardships beyond description. I have heard of a scout who got lost during his mission, and finally made it back on his own after ten days or so. But at the moment he arrived at the gate of the camp, he fell down dead. Lieutenant Matsunaga, you remained standing while you told us of your remarkable experience. You must have undergone extra hard training at the Naval Academy."

"I guess I am under some strain to avoid being laughed at by army personnel for committing a blunder. If I had visited a naval unit instead, I might have fallen down with a thud, sir."

"You are an honest man, Lieutenant Matsunaga. I think your response is only human. We are going out on an offensive expedition within a few days. You are more than welcome to the items you mentioned awhile ago. There is no need to return them to us. If there is anything else you need, please don't hesitate to let us know."

"Colonel Hidaka, the Japanese Army and Navy have been said to be on the outs. Before I came over here, I was very much concerned about what sort of treatment I would receive from you. I deeply appreciate your kind consideration from the bottom of my heart, sir."

"Putting jurisdictional disputes in Tokyo aside, in the forward areas we have a sense of brotherhood and we share equally what we have. Before I was transferred to the Philippines, I fought in the Solomons in one place after another. During that time, I became indebted to the navy for much assistance and cooperation, for I was well cared for. Lieutenant Matsunaga, please don't hesitate to accept our offer."

"It's very kind of you to say so, sir. I don't know how we could ever adequately thank you for the army units that assisted us since last night. Please send our best regards to these units through your headquarters. Thank you once again, Colonel Hidaka."

Then I returned to the quay. The warehouses near the quay, which had been used to store coconuts, were allocated to accommodate our boat unit crew.

That afternoon the senior officer assembled all hands in the billet, and gave us the following instruction:

"Captain Kubota shared the fate of the *Natori* calmly. I believe his departed soul protected us so that we had this narrow escape. We all have overcome extreme difficulty and have had an invaluable firsthand experience. I want all hands to enhance the spirit of loyalty, regain your health, and soon resume your duties in the navy."

Clothing and provisions presented by the army unit were delivered that day and everyone was looking forward to the supper, as they could eat to their fill for the first time since our disaster.

The supper was long in coming, and then we were astonished to find only a bit of thin rice gruel in teacups. No side dishes whatsoever! I instantaneously looked at the table of the PT boat crews, who were doing justice to their dinner of rice and accompanying dishes. I could not stand such unfair treatment and I blew my top.

"Go get Mr. Togawa, bear a hand!" I shouted out. The temporary medical corps officer reported to me on the double.

"Mr. Togawa, by your request, I've scrounged more than enough food from the army. Now, look! The PT boat crews over there are having a square meal while all we have is nothing but a bit of thin rice gruel. Why should I put up with this discrimination, sir?"

He replied with composure, "Lieutenant Matsunaga, do you recall I requested to be designated the medical corps officer of your boat unit this morning, sir?"

"I do, but what has that got to do with this?"

"I would like you to think through the situation calmly. Although you lack symptoms, you are all in serious straits. Remember, you haven't eaten a full meal for twelve days. Supposing you had a full meal tonight. What would you expect tomorrow? All of you would be dead by the morning. Please allow me to look after the health care of the *Natori* boat unit crew."

"Okay, dismissed."

Although I spoke to him as a superior, to be honest, I could not respond to Mr. Togawa's words with good reason. Not knowing what to do with my raised fist, I passed the word to the men to assemble.

"All hands, hear this. For the past twelve days we have been thinking nothing but food. I know you were disappointed and mad during supper tonight because it was only a cup of thin rice gruel. I also blew my stack and sent for Lieutenant Togawa, our new medical corps officer. But I found out I was in the wrong.

"When I was a boy thirteen years old, I suffered from typhoid fever. In those days, there were no medicines for it and the only treatment was to fast for about half a month. But no one died during the fast. Instead, those who died from typhoid fever were the ones who ate a lot when they were getting better.

"We will not enjoy this starvation cure, but after eating very little food for twelve days, this is what we must do. Because no one in the medical corps department of our ship has survived, I have asked Lieutenant Togawa to be our medical corps officer. He is now fully responsible for the health care of all hands. Unless otherwise granted by Lieutenant Togawa, you will not eat nor drink anything. Is that clear?"

In the days that followed there was no dispute between Mr. Togawa and our men.

Mr. Togawa's examination revealed that ten men were seriously ill and in urgent need of hospitalization. Because there was no naval hospital in Surigao, they were sent to the army hospital, where they were received warmly.

37

August 31–September 1
Conversations and Reflections

This was our first full day on shore, and we experienced a variety of emotions. The full impact of having reached our goal and our rescue by the army vessel finally hit us. A great sense of relief came over us, and we relaxed with a sense of fulfillment and joy. Being able to stretch our arms and legs was a welcome change, and this exercise, along with plenty of sleep, greatly relieved our fatigue. At the same time we experienced a sense of restlessness and uncertainty about the future.

That day we also received the sad news that one of the men sent to the army hospital the previous day had died.

Throughout the day there were many conversations among the men. I overheard an interesting conversation between Warrant Officer Heiichi Sakaguchi and Petty Officer Toshie Hatakeyama during which they reflected on our journey.

They said that before we began our voyage toward the Philippines, the senior officer, Lieutenant Kobayashi, told the men that we would reach an area patrolled by friendly small airplanes within a week, and that the group could expect to reach shore in a little more than ten days. When they saw a small airplane on the seventh day, as he had predicted, they were convinced that he would never tell a lie, and determined to do whatever he asked, no matter how difficult. They decided to entrust our lives to him.

I thought, however, that all 180 men of our boat unit felt pretty much the same way these two did toward the senior officer. I knew, too, that if he had not been with us I would have been the senior officer according to the naval code of succession and execution of command. To be honest, I doubt that I would have had the wisdom to predict seeing a small airplane. Once again I was keenly aware that we were all very fortunate that we could work under such an outstanding senior officer as Lieutenant Kobayashi.

By the next day we had already regained considerable strength, and scheduled simple daily routine work for the men, such as setting and cleaning the tables and cleaning up the billets. At 1130, the senior officer commended some of the enlisted men for their good conduct during the voyage, including seven men in the leading boat, four in the second boat, and six in the third boat.

Since June 1942, the tide had turned against Japan, and difficult days had fallen on us. More and more of us had the misfortune to lose their ships. The *Natori* was my third ship to go down. The administrative officer, Lt. (jg) Keiji Shiraishi, had been rescued after drifting at sea for two weeks after his ship, the destroyer *Amatsukaze*, was badly damaged in the South China Sea in April 1944, so lost his ship twice in the same year.

The assistant navigator, Ensign Hoshino, was attached to the *Kuma*, a light cruiser, when it was sunk by an enemy submarine off the coast of Penang, an island off the northwest coast of the Malay peninsula in January 1944. He had to swim for five hours before he was rescued.

The second division officer, Lieutenant Kubo, told us about Leading Seaman Takeda's decision after the disaster. Lieutenant Kubo and his messenger, Takeda, were in the last group to get into the water when the *Natori* sank. As they swam to the No. 1 launch, they found it already loaded with survivors. Then they swam for about twenty minutes to the No. 1 boat, where Lieutenant Kubo got into the boat, but Takeda kept holding onto a log and refused to get into the boat, no matter how often the men in the boat urged him on.

"A raft suits me well," he said, swimming toward a raft in the distance. In that raging sea, Takeda had taken the trouble to escort his division officer to a boat. But Leading Seaman Nakamura, a buddy of Takeda who had joined the navy with him, told about an episode in Takeda's naval experience that put a different slant on the story. When the light cruiser *Tenryu* went down in December 1942, Takeda got into one of the boats, which for some reason capsized, and only a few of the men survived. He was one of the survivors, yet this sad experience may have held him back from getting aboard the No. 1 boat.

One conversation I recall involved three officers, each of whom was in a different boat. The electrical division officer, Ensign Muraoka, was contrasting the relationship between crew members while on board ship compared with those that prevailed in the boats. On board ship, he noted, men were classified as active service, reenlisted, draftees, ex–teacher draftees, boy–sailors, and others; occupational categories ranged from sailors (gunnery, torpedo, navigation, and communications) to engineers (main engines, boiler, electrical, auxiliary engines, and construction) to medics to clerks and to supply personnel. Sometimes, on board ship, these classifications and departmental groups were antagonistic to one another. Also, there were seven ratings among the enlisted men, beginning with Seaman Second Class up to Petty Officer Superior Class. It was rare for an enlisted man to speak with another crew member of a different rating in a different department. In the boat, however, such distinctions by classification, occupation, and rate disappeared and all hands worked together as a group.

The second division officer, Lieutenant Kubo, said what distinguished the third boat from others was that a reserve officer played a significant role throughout the voyage. Lieutenant Kubo had once instructed reserve ensigns at the gunnery school at Tateyam, and he didn't have a good impression of them. But this experience with Ens. Hisao Shozawa, who was out of the third reserve officers training course and taking passage on the *Natori* to Palau Island, was quite different. Lieutenant Kubo was concerned that Ensign Shozawa might be ostracized by the *Natori's* survivors if he pulled rank on them.

As it was, Ensign Shozawa put aside any sense of privilege, such as being an officer or a passenger. He mingled with the boat crew, and was always the first to undertake any hardships. Lieutenant Kubo was afraid that Ensign Shozawa would exhaust himself, but he probably was an athlete in his school days, for he held out until the boat unit landed. The morale of the third boat was much higher than that of the other two boats, partly because of Ensign Shozawa's strenuous efforts.

The paymaster made these observations about the second boat. Officers are classified as graduates of the three Naval Academies (the Naval Academy, the Naval Engineering Academy, and the Naval Paymaster's Academy), the Higher Merchant Marine

Schools (Tokyo and Kobe), universities (permanent duty, two-year term, reserve officers), and special service officers, such as mustangs (those who rose to officer status from enlisted status). But in the boat unit, such disparities no longer existed. One reserve ensign in the second boat had a most active part with the boat crew.

On board ship, there were some instances when officers did not get along well with enlisted men or with other officers, but in the boats all the previous differences and distinctions disappeared and we worked in great harmony, a major factor in making our voyage so successful.

Paymaster Lieutenant Imai and I carried on the following conversation about the successful return of our boat unit:

I mentioned that I thought that those from the districts along the Sea of Japan had dispositions different from those from other parts of Japan. On the first night we began rowing toward the Philippines, the oarsmen were not used to rowing in pairs, and we did not make much progress. I then suggested to the senior officer that the working hours be extended until we covered thirty miles, the planned distance for each day. But he turned down my idea. A man like myself, from Kyushu, the southwesternmost island, tended to work really hard for a short time, but was not suited to persevere and bear hardships for a lengthy time.

The senior officer was from Niigata prefecture, along the Sea of Japan, and most of the men were from Aomori to Shimane prefectures, the northern and western prefectures along the Sea of Japan. By nature the senior officer was broad-minded and patient, not irritable, and inspired others to bear hardships. One of the factors leading to the successful return of our boat unit was the disposition of those from these districts.

The paymaster had been associated with Lieutenant Kobayashi, the navigator, as a colleague of his own age on the *Natori*, and had not thought of him as an especially respected person. But once the navigator assumed the command and became the senior officer, he showed strong leadership, proceeding to the Philippines despite everyone else's opposition, and under circumstances in which it would be impossible to redo a mistake. Even though the men were all against the senior officer's decision to proceed to the Philippines, once the decision was made, they rowed with all their might. The brilliant command and leadership of the senior officer and the outstanding obedience of his men went hand in hand, and led to the success of the voyage.

Mr. Hoshino, the assistant navigator, also appreciated the

senior officer. "No matter how afflicted or bitter I felt during the voyage," he said, "when I looked at the senior officer's demeanor and conduct, I kept telling myself that we must achieve our goal at any cost."

After landing, I learned that the crew of either the second or third boat tried to catch fish by using a naval ensign for a fishing net. It certainly was outrageous for anyone to try to catch fish with a sacred ensign, and as the officer responsible for military discipline, I thought of cracking down on their misbehavior. However, it was "the day after the fair," and I decided to think it over before taking any disciplinary action.

A commanding officer is responsible for providing his men sufficient food to maintain the fighting strength of the military forces. Could I really, as the second in command, say that I had provided enough food to maintain the fighting strength of the *Natori* boat unit? I decided that it would be too self-centered to exercise rigid control over the crew when I had not fulfilled my own duties and responsibilities. The staff officers who had never been under fire in a battle might well have persisted in disciplining the crew, sticking stubbornly to an official code, but a battle line commander must avoid a "remedy that is worse than the disease."

In peace, military discipline takes precedence over everything else. But in wartime, shouldn't the maintenance of fighting strength be given a higher priority than military discipline?

Setting aside this as mere theory, I thought of physically showing them a substitute for a fishing net and chewing them out by saying, "Such-and-such a thing could have been used as a fishing net. Why in the world did you use a naval ensign instead?" I tried hard to think of something that could have substituted for a fishing net, but couldn't come up with any idea.

38

September 1–10
Leaving Surigao Behind

Lieutenant Togawa, who volunteered to serve as the medical corps officer of our boat unit, looked after our health with such wisdom and sensitivity that we could not thank him enough for what he had done.

One time I saw young Mr. Togawa getting up early to go out, and I praised him for being an early riser.

"I was afraid that if the hard fiber vegetables we usually get in our normal rations had been served to your crew, more than half of you would have died," he admitted. "Because we are prohibited from dealing directly with the inhabitants, I talked to the military police detachment commander, explaining the situation to him. He then had the kindness to go out with me to search for the proper food. That is why I rose early this morning."

Mr. Togawa did all this without expecting anything in return and, thanks to his noble efforts, we recovered our health much sooner than expected. Arrangements were made to transport all hands to Manila one week later on two submarine chasers.

A few days before we left for Manila, the crews of the PT boat unit and the *Natori* boat unit joined in an evening of musical entertainment and a volley ball tournament. Later the crews of the PT boat unit even threw a farewell party for us. Although there was a limited supply of food and drinks, there was true fellowship. True mutual respect and appreciation had developed between us.

The afternoon before leaving Surigao, I took a stroll along a street of the town, and stopped at the officers' club. It was run by the army, but naval officers were also welcome. Not much food or beverage was in this remote club at the front line, for supplies were no longer received from the Japanese homeland. The only thing I found there was some gaudy-looking crimson palm wine in a big glass bottle, and seeing its color, it didn't appeal to me. I then decided to relax in a sofa and rest awhile.

From this spot I could hear and observe an army second lieutenant playing the piano with enthusiasm. As he played "The Blue Danube," I was reminded of Sadatoshi Sugiura, a classmate of mine at the Naval Academy. I then spoke to the army lieutenant.

"Pardon me, sir. Matsunaga is my name. I'm a naval lieutenant. I was born and brought up in a rural district in Saga, and did not learn to appreciate music. But my classmate, Sugiura, played the piano in the Naval Academy canteen and taught me how to appreciate western music by introducing me to 'The Blue Danube.' Your performance reminded me of him. I know very few men who can play the piano. Where did you learn it?"

"I was a music teacher at an elementary school. But, I'll tell you, within a few days our outfit is going out to the central part of Mindanao to fight the guerillas there. I cannot hope to return alive, and I am ready to lay down my life. Today is my last day off, and I want to enjoy myself by playing the piano without a care in the world. Although my performance is unskilled, I'm glad to hear that it reminded you of your classmate, sir."

"It is a sensitive question as to how to kill time before going out to a battlefield where you will exchange fire with an enemy," I said. "I have no hobbies so I try to divert my mind from worries by drinking. While drinking, I forget all about the upcoming battle. But once I'm sober again, I feel even more lonesome than before. I do admire you for spending your spare time before your mission by being absorbed in playing the piano. In my heart, I pray for your good luck in the battle."

On our final night in Surigao, Lieutenant Togawa and I decided to have a walk along its beautiful shoreline, which was dotted with palm groves. The silvery moon added to the beauty of the scene. As we walked, I told him of the unforgettable conversation I had at the officers' club that afternoon.

"I am glad to hear such a wonderful story. Even in the army, there are persons of great character.

"Mr. Togawa, our relationship has involved life and death, for without you the lives of 180 men could not have been saved. After we part tomorrow, we may never see each other again. I'd like to be personal friends, apart from our military association."

"That's more than I could ask for. Then I could have a heart-to-heart talk with you, Mr. Matsunaga."

"Incidentally, Togawa-san, do you recall what happened on the evening of the day we arrived here? All you let us have was a cup of thin rice gruel, while you had a square meal. I was so mad at you that I was ready to stab you to death, depending on your reply to my question."

"I perceived your intent from the furious look on your face. That's why I kept my distance. It was a lucky thing that you had a case of typhoid fever before. Otherwise, I bet, the issue would have been a lot more serious, Matsunaga-san."

"On that night, Togawa-san, as I thought it over in bed, I realized that your volunteering to be medical corps officer of our boat unit was a scheme to enable you to do what was best for us. In a way you risked your own neck, when you, as a young surgeon lieutenant, schemed against an older line lieutenant.

"When I saw that all of you were suffering from starvation, I also realized that I could not persuade you of the seriousness of your condition. So, I decided that the only way to do what was best for you was to be designated your medical corps officer. Please forgive me if you're angry.

"During our basic training at the Naval Medical School, Superintendent Tohei Sasagawa challenged us. `Young as you are, you are all medical experts, and you must take pride and exercise discernment in your professional practice. No issue will arise as long as you work under a superior who respects you as a competent professional. But if your superior is the kind of person who lords it over you, and tells you to do what is not sound medical practice, how would you deal with him? I want you to be prepared at all times for the worst situation. That's why I boldly decided to scheme against you, Matsunaga-san."*

"Togawa-san, I am very much impressed with your story. As

---

*The words of Superintendent Sasagawa—"If your superior tells you to do what is not sound medical practice ... "—influenced the young medical corps officers to a great extent, and gave them a guideline to follow not only while they served in the navy, but also throughout their lives. After the war, they published a book, *Mr. Tohei,* out of their respect and affection for him.

you know, in the Japanese Navy, an average line officer would tell you that absolute obedience is required to a line officer's orders. But Superintendent Sasagawa trained you the other way around, and gave you an extraordinary new perspective, and you schemed against me according to this training. As a result, you saved the lives of more than 180 men. It is a most impressive story."

"Matsunaga-san, I myself also had a valuable experience. To be honest with you, when I went down to the quay to meet your boat unit, I expected to find all the crew members near their last breath. This is what we would expect medically, considering your lack of food and water for twelve days and the hardships you endured. In fact, we could expect many to collapse and die the moment they reached a safe zone. But, surprisingly, the crew was maintaining strict military discipline and acting as a unit. It was well organized under the leadership of the senior officer, Lieutenant Kobayashi, who I believe was the source of their will to live," said Lieutenant Togawa.

"I received a liberal education throughout my high school and university days, and developed a negative attitude toward military discipline," he continued. "I came to regard it as an evil that completely deprived persons of their freedom. But seeing the well-organized and orderly discipline of the crew of the *Natori* boat unit, I have changed my view on military discipline. It is not always evil, but in reality has many good aspects."

"When I visited the Army Headquarters for negotiation, Colonel Hidaka told me of a scout missing for over ten days. On his return to the camp, having survived all sorts of hardships, he fell dead the moment he entered the gate of the camp," I said. "The colonel then commended me for standing while I reported on our voyage, though I could not explain, even to myself, why I was able to do so in my feeble condition."

"Matsunaga-san, when you went to the Army Headquarters all by yourself you were conscious of being the second in command of the *Natori* boat unit. I'm sure it was that consciousness that motivated you and enabled you to keep standing. A human being may be a weak creature by himself, but he is much stronger when part of an organization."

"Togawa-san, that is an interesting observation. It is hard to tell if either of us will be able to return to the Japanese homeland. If one of us returns home, let him visit the family of the other at a convenient time. I am Ichiro Matsunaga from Saga prefecture, a member of the 68th class of the Naval Academy. You can ask some graduates of the academy about the whereabouts of my family."

"I'm from Tokyo, and Kiyohiko Togawa is my name. I graduated from the medical department of Tokyo Imperial University in 1943. Through an inquiry to my alma mater, you can learn where my family lives."

We then shook hands firmly, as new friends, with mutual respect and trust.

On the following morning the *Natori* boat unit crew boarded two submarine chasers bound for Manila. As almost a hundred officers and men were aboard each small vessel, they were overflowing with passengers. It was a heartwarming experience to be seen off by the PT boat crews and the army personnel. We bid farewell to Surigao with many satisfying memories.

Soon we encountered an oncoming ship, which turned out to be the No. 3 Armed Transport, the ship we were traveling with when we met disaster. She was still on the active list and appeared to be carrying out a new mission. The senior officer sent a message by semaphore to her.

"From *Natori* navigator, Lieutenant Kobayashi. *Natori* went down at the point where it incurred the torpedo attack. Captain Kubota shared the fate with his ship. The *Natori* boat unit of 180 officers and men arrived at Surigao on our own, and is now on its way to a new assignment. Wish you and your ship the fortunes of war."

The No. 3 Armed Transport replied. "Wish the *Natori* ship's company every happiness and good health." It was an emotional moment as we waved farewell. Only one month ago the *Natori* steamed along this same course connecting Hinatuan Passage, Cebu Island, and Manila.

We saw much more movement of land troops than before, which seemed to indicate that an attack by U.S. forces was anticipated. We also realized that enemy submarines could be under these waters, yet we were not attacked along the way, probably because they considered it a waste of torpedoes to attack submarine chasers.

In Manila Bay I saw only a few ships in the anchorage, much fewer than one month ago. On the other hand the number of wrecked ships showing their red bottoms had increased considerably.

In reply to the dispatch we had sent to the Navy Department regarding the arrival of the *Natori* boat unit in Manila, the officers of the unit holding the rank of lieutenant or higher were ordered to report to the Navy Department in Tokyo by air as soon as the situation permitted. Arrangements had been made at the Fleet Headquarters for us to take passage on a Type II flying boat, which was bound for Yokohama via Taitung, Formosa, on the following morning.

That day I chanced to meet my classmate, Lt. Uichi Komai, at the 31st Naval Base near the Manila Pier, who told me the No. 3 Armed Transport was lost in the southern waters off Mindanao Island. Remembering the days when she accompanied the *Natori*, I prayed in my heart for the safety of Captain Hamamoto and the ship's company.

I wondered whether I should call First Secretary Takagi at the Japanese Embassy and explain to him the reason I would not be able to deliver the snapshot of his son to his father-in-law, Vice Admiral Itoh. I realized that if I called him, however, the *Natori's* sinking would be revealed, and this was not permitted, so I decided to leave for home without getting in touch with him and gave up this important social duty.

That night I stayed at the Manila Hotel, which overlooked the whole of Manila Bay. It was a top-notch hotel, and some said that Gen. Douglas MacArthur was very fond of it. The sunset I saw that evening was spectacular, but it was no match for the ones I had seen from the boat far out in the ocean.

Early the following morning, four cars were dispatched to the hotel to pick up our group of six officers; a fully armed sailor was in each car. They said that if any of the cars broke down on the way they would desert it on the spot, and proceed in the other cars, which was why four cars were dispatched. Judging from this, I realized the wisdom of the senior officer when he made special efforts to avoid an encounter with guerillas as we neared shore a few weeks ago.

Our cars ran along the east coast of Manila Bay to Cavite Naval Base, where the flying boat had already completed its engine run-up and was awaiting our arrival. To avoid a morning air raid by the enemy, our plane took off in the darkness without waiting for dawn to break in the eastern sky. As we winged our way over the South China Sea, my mind overflowed with countless emotions and memories of this lifesaving, life-changing experience.

39

August 29–September 26
Reality and Renewal in Australia

The *Hardhead* continued to patrol the area off Surigao Strait until September 14. After our August 28 contact with a destroyer, we had no further sightings or contact with enemy ships, though we had many contacts with enemy aircraft. On August 31 we had our first, though relatively minor, attack by an enemy aircraft. That morning we sighted aircraft two or three times, and dove on each occasion. About 1430 a floatplane was sighted about four miles away flying directly toward us. We dove immediately, and four minutes later, when we were at a depth of two hundred feet, we heard an explosion, apparently from a depth bomb. This was a poignant reminder that an enemy was seeking us out, and that the lack of countermeasures we had experienced must not lead to complacency.

Another hazard we faced from time to time was mines that had broken loose from their anchors and were now floating in the water. If a ship or submarine contacted one of the "horns" on the mine, it would detonate and probably sink the vessel, so we usually tried to explode or sink these mines with gunfire.

On August 31 we sighted such a mine, and the following quotation from the patrol report summarizes the action we took:

1707. Sighted floating mine (four horns, round and

covered with sea growth). Commenced circling and shooting. Fired two pans 20 mm; no hits (500 yard range). Broke out rifles and closed range to 350 yards; ship had a pretty bad roll for machine gun fire with tracer control. Six hits with the rifles but mine still floating. Broke out .30 cal. machine guns and sprayed the mine from 300 yards. Several more hits out of 500 rounds.

1908. Headed north with mine still floating. Anyhow, tested all machine guns and found out who were the shooters and who were the talkers.

On the evening of September 5 another experience served as a powerful reminder of the need for careful attention and diligence in the operation of the boat. At dusk, as we prepared to patrol on the surface during a moonlit night, the captain ordered that the ballast tanks be partly flooded so that we would ride lower in the water to present a smaller silhouette, just as we did the night we attacked the *Natori*. This involved opening the vents on the ballast tanks for a very brief period while cruising along on the surface. Somehow, the vents were left open too long, and the bow of the boat went under water and we started to submerge–all this without sounding the diving alarm, closing the valve in the ventilation system, or clearing the bridge!

Fortunately, those on watch throughout the boat realized what was happening, and each man took the necessary steps to rectify the situation, but not before water began pouring into the ventilation system, and through the ventilation ducts into the various compartments of the boat. The crew performed exactly as they had been trained for such emergencies, and there was no significant damage except to some electronic equipment in the radio room. There was, of course, a good deal of mopping up to do.

The most embarrassing aspect of this episode was that at that exact moment, the officer on decoding duty was in the radio room, sitting under a ventilation duct, setting up the decoding device for the day. The instructions for doing this, a top secret document that gave daily directions for the entire month, was printed with ink that disappeared when it became wet. When the water came out of the ventilation duct, it landed on this document and these instructions, our only copy, disappeared in a moment! It was embarrassing to send a message to the base reporting that we could no longer decode their daily messages, and that if they wished to communicate with us, they would have to utilize a little-used backup system. This was a reminder, which we never forgot, that a submarine is a complex, sensitive, integrated machine and that safe operation of the boat requires great attention to detail.

On September 12 a totally new dimension of our work developed. A large United States Naval Task Force entered the area to begin the assault on the Philippines, and the *Hardhead* was assigned "lifeguard" duty, which involved being on the surface at a location known to all the pilots, and being prepared to rescue any pilots shot down. By knowing our location, pilots could, if necessary and possible, nurse their crippled planes as close as possible to our location before ditching, and radio their location to us.

The following morning, as we were on our lifeguard station at 0600, we sighted many U.S. planes flying westward to the Philippines. On several occasions pairs of planes circled us, but for reasons we did not understand, we could not communicate with them. Shortly before 1000, two planes circled us, flew off to the southeast, came back and circled us again, and again flew off in the same direction. We assumed they were trying to lead us in that direction to a downed pilot. We set out immediately to the southeast, but found nothing.

About 1040 that morning we sighted the masts of the task force, and heard a plane report us as a "friendly submarine," giving the correct range and bearing from the task force. This was encouraging to us, for submarines always had a concern that some U.S. pilot might not have gotten the word, and failed to identify them as a "friendly submarine." One U.S. submarine was sunk by a U.S. plane through such a mishap.

Although we did not rescue any pilots at this time, on our next patrol, on the west coast of the Philippines, we rescued two downed pilots. One was a miraculous rescue in which, in the dark of night, we "stumbled" across a raft carrying the pilot, Comdr. Fred Bakutis, commander of all the fighter planes on the *Enterprise*, six and a half days after he was shot down. The other rescued pilot was a young ensign of the same ship, whom we had aboard within two hours after his plane went down, because his wing man flew over, informing us of his location, some twenty miles away.

On September 14 we rendezvoused with the USS *Gar*, the submarine that was to relieve us in the area. After giving the captain of the *Gar* information on the area, we headed for the southern boundary of the area en route to Fremantle, West Australia, the port near Perth.

Our route took us through the Molucca Sea, where we crossed the equator on September 17, the Ceram Sea, the Banda Sea, Ombai Strait, the Savu Sea, and into the Indian Ocean. Many islands are in these areas, and though the United States had gained control of the area, many islands were still occupied by Japanese forces, who continued to fight under difficult conditions. In the Banda Sea we sighted a plane at seven miles and dove immediately. The plane dropped two depth bombs, one of which exploded close enough to us to cause a few light bulbs to break.

On the morning of September 26 we arrived off Fremantle, Western Australia. A boat pulled alongside, enabling a pilot to come aboard who would guide us into the harbor. This boat also brought us some milk, apples, and best of all, our mail.

Sixty-three days had elapsed since we left Pearl Harbor, and except for five hours on Midway Island, we had been at sea for the entire period, and had traveled some fourteen thousand miles. It was exciting to come into a friendly port and we looked forward to the experiences that awaited us in Australia. After arriving in port, the entire crew would have a two-week rest period at hotels that had been taken over for this purpose by the U.S. Navy.

As we moored alongside the USS *Batfish*, we carried a broom tied to the mast, the traditional way a submarine indicated that it had achieved a "clean sweep." Although we had sunk only one ship, the patrol had been a major success because this ship was a battleship. A small band, composed of navy personnel, was playing on the waterfront to welcome us and celebrate our safe return. The division commander came aboard to welcome us and to congratulate Captain McMaster and the crew on a successful patrol.

Soon, however, we learned that another submarine, the USS *Stingray*, in passing through the area about fourteen days after our encounter with the enemy, had come across and rescued four Japanese sailors adrift in a rubber raft, and had brought them to Australia. Interrogation revealed that they had been crew members on the light cruiser *Natori*, which had sunk on August 18 after being hit by one torpedo. The clear conclusion was, therefore, that the ship we had sunk was this light cruiser, and not a battleship.

What deflating news! Although we had not talked much about it, we had all visualized the honors we would receive for sinking a battleship–probably a Navy Cross for Captain McMaster and a Presidential Unit Citation for the crew. And now, only a light cruiser! If we ourselves had concluded the ship we sank was a light cruiser, we would have still considered this a very significant accomplishment. But in our disappointment, our accomplishment seemed trivial.

Then we began to reflect on the sequence of events. One torpedo hit? In our first attack we had clear evidence of two hits. And in our second attack, when the ship was essentially dead in the water, we had clear evidence of six hits. And then we remembered that one of the lookouts had reported an explosion on the far side of the target toward the second ship. Could it be that the second ship was a light cruiser that had received one hit, and did this explain its erratic behavior after the attack? This would leave the main target as a battleship that sank only after receiving at least eight hits. This was the only way we could explain the events we had observed and experienced.

With these speculations in mind we went off to our rest period. We officers were assigned a small country hotel, a few miles out of Perth, that could accommodate twenty-five or thirty persons. What a delightful rest period! During the last weeks of our patrol the meals had been adequate at best. I still recall the waitress at my first Australian breakfast saying in a lovely accent, "We have steak and eggs for breakfast." What a treat! I especially enjoyed playing tennis with Australians at a small, local tennis club where I was cordially welcomed, and meeting with the Inter Varsity Christian Fellowship group at the University of Western Australia.

From time to time, however, we did return to the question of what ship (or ships) we had sunk. We were convinced (or perhaps convinced ourselves) that the main target had been a battleship, and that someday, when the war ended and all the facts were in, our conviction would be vindicated. We maintained this conviction during the five subsequent war patrols the *Hardhead* made, and talked about it from time to time.

There was one unexpected consequence of this matter. Captain McMaster, a fine person and a capable naval officer, had, an unfortunate incident during our rest period. In a conversation with the admiral and division commander and their staffs, he continued to insist that it was a battleship that we had sunk. The conversation got out of hand, and within a day Captain McMaster was relieved of command of the *Hardhead*. It was a tragedy, for the issue was really not that momentous, and the facts would certainly have come out in due time. That was all that really mattered.

Despite the unsettling development regarding Captain McMaster and the ship we had sunk, the rest period provided a wonderful opportunity for renewal of body, mind, and spirit. I had time to reflect on the experiences of our first war patrol, and realized that I had grown in maturity, confidence, and the ability to assume major responsibilities. I began to think about my life and the career I would follow when I returned home. I also realized that we would face dangers, and possibly death, as we continued making war patrols. But in all these thoughts there was a deepening dependence on God, and any anxieties were overbalanced by a sense of confidence and anticipation for our second war patrol and what lay beyond.

Epilogue
HIJMS Natori
Ichiro Matsunaga

After the war, when the hardships of that era were over, the very first thing that I wanted to do was to learn what had become of the launch and the rubber raft separated from us at the scene of the disaster. I also made a study of the rescue operations that had been carried out to search for the *Natori* crew. I learned the following about these matters:

After the *Natori* had been hit by the enemy submarine's torpedo, the captain ordered that urgent dispatches be sent out. The first dispatch, sent at 0330, was as follows:

"0240 August 18. Torpedoed by enemy submarine. One hit. Lat. 12° 05′ N, Lon. 129° 26′ E. Despite serious damage, no fear of sinking at present. Unable to maneuver." The second dispatch, sent at 0530: "Getting under way westward at six knots, under own power."

Upon receipt of these dispatches, the Fleet Headquarters in Manila ordered various units to take action. These are the orders that were given:

"Discontinue transport of supplies by *Natori*. Bring her back to Philippines under escort of No. 3 Armed Transport."

"Unit of 154th Air Group remaining in Manila and Air Group unit in Tacloban shall escort *Natori* with as many planes as may be spared."

"1. *Kiyoshimo* and *Take* [destroyers] shall, without delay, put to sea and rendezvous with *Natori* unit.

2. After rendezvous, *Kiyoshimo* shall take command of No. 3 Armed Transport, and resume transport mission to Palau.

3. *Take* shall escort *Natori* and bring her back to Manila.

211

4.   *Uranami* [destroyer] shall immediately shove off from Cebu to join *Natori* unit, and escort them to San Bernardino Strait."

Headquarters in Manila allocated all operable ships to the rescue operations for the *Natori* crew. But earlier, the commanding officers of the *Natori* and the No. 3 Armed Transport had made this prearrangement:

"Judging from the circumstances, this will probably be the last mission to Palau. Should either one of us incur damage during the voyage, the undamaged ship shall forsake the damaged ship and her crew, and continue the mission to Palau." The No. 3 Armed Transport, therefore, proceeded to Palau according to this prearrangement, leaving the damaged *Natori* and her crew behind at the scene.

On August 19, the following day, a search plane, a medium-attack bomber of the 761st Air Group stationed at Legaspi, Luzon Island, spotted the *Natori's* survivors, and dispatched an urgent message.

"Observed one launch, three boats, numerous rafts. 100° 350 miles from Legaspi. 1035."

For some odd reason, eleven precious hours elapsed before the rescue ships began their assigned tasks as given by the dispatches from the Fleet Headquarters.

At 0700 on August 19, the destroyer *Urakaze*, the flagship of the 19th Destroyer Division, arrived at the scene of the *Natori's* disaster. Then, the *Kiyoshimo* and *Take* arrived there at 0900. These three destroyers, directed by the 19th Destroyer Division commander, searched for survivors of the *Natori* all day long. Unfortunately, finding no clues of the disaster, they decided to return to Cebu for the time being.

About 2100, the dispatch from the search plane was belatedly relayed to these destroyers. They immediately made a 180° turn, reversed course, put all engines on the line, and hastened back to the scene of the disaster. At the same time, the Fleet Headquarters passed this word:

"Rescue *Natori's* survivors spotted by 761st Air Group medium-attack bomber. Air Groups at Legaspi and Tacloban shall commence searching for survivors and antisubmarine patrol beginning early morning of August 20."

The three destroyers arrived, for the second time, at the scene of the *Natori's* disaster at 0700 on August 20, and immediately began searching for the survivors. Because of stormy weather, however, the search was extremely difficult. In addition, the search plane saw no sign of the survivors from the air, and the *Kiyoshimo* abandoned the search to resume her original mission, and headed for Palau.

The light cruiser *Kinu* and the destroyer *Shigure* had accomplished their transport missions to Palau and were on their way back to Cebu, and arrived at the scene at 1420 on August 20, joining the *Urakaze* and the *Take*, already engaged in the search. Commanded by the *Kinu's* captain, the four ships energetically searched for the survivors, but none of them could find any clue. Moreover, they were running short on fuel, and they discontinued the search and left the scene at 2020. The search by air was continued after that, but there was no further success, and it was terminated on August 23.

The *Natori's* sinking took place in the Pacific Ocean, three hundred miles equidistant from Palau and Cebu. At that time, enemy vessels and aircraft were operating extensively nearby, and the possibility of more disasters had to be considered. Yet the light cruiser *Kinu* and the three destroyers searched for the survivors of the *Natori* for as long as two days, despite the dangers involved.

From the few airplanes on hand, the Air Groups managed to allocate search planes for one week, day in and day out. However, despite the devoted efforts made by all concerned, they could not rescue the survivors of the *Natori*.

The rubber raft, with the assistant recognition officer and five others aboard, was cast loose from the No. 2 boat in the storm about midnight of August 18, the day the *Natori* sank, with plans to accommodate them in the No. 2 boat on the following day. The storm continued all day on August 19, and they remained in the raft. When the storm was over and the sea subsided on August 20, we searched diligently for them, but they were nowhere to be seen.

For those on the rubber raft, fasting began immediately, for the raft carried nothing to eat or drink. They caught rain with their caps and appeased their thirst, but could not save what they caught without a container. They had no oars in the raft, and there was nothing they could do but to pray to God that they might be carried to the Philippines by the current. After a week, two of them became insane and died on the tenth day.

During this time, sharks attacked the rubber raft and bit off one side of it, causing air to leak out. They were very much concerned about another attack, in which case the raft might no longer sustain the weight of six men. Thanks to God, nothing happened to make the situation worse.

About the twelfth day, they became completely exhausted and were as good as dead. Finally, the assistant recognition officer fell into a coma. On August 31, on the fourteenth day, they were sighted by the submarine USS *Stingray* and rescued. The assistant recognition officer and three other survivors were sent to the POW camp in Brisbane, Australia, via a hospital in Port Darwin. The war ended while they were in Brisbane.

In regard to the launch that became separated from us, an ensign aboard filled me in on what happened:

1st day: Requested towing by a boat. The leading boat passed the word to throw over a sea anchor. As there was no sea anchor in the launch, we drifted leeward rapidly, and lost sight of the boat unit in the afternoon. The storm became furious in the evening.

2d day: Light rain. The sea was still raging. In the morning we saw a medium-attack bomber overhead and semaphored that we were the *Natori* crew. Our message was acknowledged.

3d day: The wind and rain subsided, but the visibility was still low. In the afternoon, a reconnaissance seaplane flew over and recognized us.

4th day: Fair. Though there were swells, the wind and waves greatly decreased. Twenty-one-year-old Ens. Meisei Naramura took command of the launch as senior officer present. Because we no longer expected rescue ships, he decided we could proceed to the Philippines on our own. We made fourteen oars out of the wainscot of the launch, and figured we would reach shore in ten days or so if we proceeded westward, knowing that we would be carried in this direction by the North Equatorial Current. As for food, we ate one small ship's biscuit a day.

5th day: We suffered much more from thirst than from hunger. We were cautious not to make noise or talk loudly, as enemy submarines might be operating nearby.

6th day: We were dying for drinking water and when someone said water in the deep sea has less salt content, we managed to scoop some up, but found it just as salty as the water near the surface.

7th day: We encountered a severe rainsquall, which quenched our thirst. But we had a terrible time bailing water out of the launch.

8th day: Fair. Some were so thirsty that they could not resist drinking their own urine. Everyone was encouraged when someone said we would sight an island the next day.

9th–17th day: Mostly clear days. Rainsqualls came once every two days. A cloud appeared to be an island, but we were discouraged when it turned out to be a cloud, an experience repeated several times in succeeding days. We became short on food, and from the tenth day on, we observed a new rule of one biscuit per two days.

18th day: Fair. We became so feeble and weak that hardly anyone could row. A medium–attack bomber flew over, but did not recognize us. Up to this time, we sat upright and saluted with a deep bow toward the Imperial Palace every morning. Now half of us could not sit upright any longer.

20th day: Fair. Stoker Petty Officer First Class Akita died from exhaustion, the first victim of this ordeal. Beginning about the tenth day, some began to blurt out such incredible things as "Oh, I see the lights of Yokosuka" or suddenly jump into the water. From this day on, we had one or two men die every day.

21st day: Fair. Ensign Fukunaga died. We saw a small bird flying nearby, and saw some floats, such as coconut shells and seaweeds, which made everyone happy to realize that land was not too far away. We ate some crabs as small as grains of rice attached to the floats. A B–24 circled overhead, which seemed to recognize the launch.

22d day: Though we sighted reconnaissance seaplane, they did not recognize us. We were mad at this friendly plane, because it was poorer than the enemy plane in spotting us.

24th day: About 2000, a hospital ship, illuminating big red crosses, passed about five thousand meters from us. Because we had no light in the launch, we shouted as loudly as we possibly could, but the ship did not hear us. We felt so feeble that hardly anyone could rise. Almost everyone lay down on the bottom of the launch all day.

26th day (September 12): Cloudy. Low visibility. Early in the morning, we were spotted by a formation of four U.S. F6F's. To the south, we observed a fleet of twenty to thirty vessels, including battleships and aircraft carriers, and about as many in another fleet to the north. Soon, a destroyer came to our rescue. At the beginning of our drifting, there were fifty-three personnel aboard the launch. Of the total, twelve died during the period we drifted; the forty-one survivors were sent to Camp McCoy in Wisconsin until the end of the war.

In June 1944, when the U.S. invasion forces swarmed the Mariana Islands, the Japanese Navy stopped sending reinforcements to these waters. Then, suspecting that the next decisive battles would take place in the Philippine Islands, reinforcements were sent to the Palaus, where a preliminary skirmish was likely to take place. The United States completed mopping–up operations in the Marianas in August, and the time for a decisive battle for the Philippines was rapidly approaching. The United States positioned its submarines in the Philippine waters, and in August airplanes based in the Marianas began reconnaissance flights over these waters. The large fleets observed from the launch were probably the striking forces for Leyte Island.

After the war ended I lived in Sasebo City, Nagasaki prefecture. There is a U.S. naval base in this city, and on several occasions I exchanged greetings with the U.S. Navy personnel. A captain told me his story. At the outbreak of the war, he was attached to a destroyer defending Cavite Naval Base in Manila. When they received a warning about an anticipated Japanese invasion, they cleared hastily to the South China Sea. After his ship was sunk by an enemy assault, he was rescued by the Japanese Navy while drifting on a raft.

Then I told him my story about the *Natori* boat unit, and our three hundred–mile voyage in the waters off the east coast of the Philippine Islands. As he listened he repeatedly remarked "wonderful," and when I finished he expressed admiration for the practical training we had received, and for Lieutenant Kobayashi and the superb command and leadership he gave during the voyage. There was neither a winner's arrogance nor a loser's servility. I said sympathetically to him that he must have had a very difficult experience in the cold westerly monsoon that prevails in the South China Sea in December. He responded compassionately to me, saying that I must have been scorched in the Philippine waters in August. Although we were complete strangers before our conversation, we shook our hands firmly as though we had been acquainted with each other for many years.

As I reflected on our conversation, I realized the truth of the saying, "The navies of the great powers may at times engage in battles with each other at the request of their countries, but in peacetime, they are good companions having a common foe called Nature."

Several historic voyages have been made in small boats after a disaster at sea.

In April 1789, as the HMS *Bounty* of the Royal Navy was traveling near the Fiji Islands, the executive officer and many crew members conspired and mutinied against the captain. Capt. William

Bligh and eighteen of his right-hand men were cast adrift from the ship in a small launch, only twenty-three feet long.

For navigation equipment, they were allowed to take a compass, sextant, and navigation almanac. For food, they had about 150 pounds of biscuit, 20 pounds of pork, 30 gallons of water, and some rum, wine, and bread. Captain Bligh was eager to gain revenge on the traitors, and decided to proceed to Timor Island, an anchorage for many European ships. On the forty-second day, after navigating thirty-seven hundred miles, they landed on this island.

In October 1870, the USS *Saginaw*, searching for a wrecked ship, ran aground on a reef near Ocean Island, 190 miles west of Midway. The ninety-three men in the ship's company were able to take many provisions out of the wreckage, and they were not in needy circumstances for the time being.

Unfortunately, Ocean Island was remote from normal shipping routes, so they could not expect a ship to come to their help, and in those days there was no radio communication. Lieutenant Talbot and four others volunteered to make the passage to Hawaii by boat, a direct distance of eighteen hundred miles, to inform the navy of the disaster. Considering the direction of prevailing winds, it was necessary to detour somewhat, and they planned to voyage twenty-five hundred miles in twenty-five days. The boat was loaded with a chronometer, aneroid barometer, sextant, compass, navigation almanac, charts, 235 feet of log line, sandglass, lantern, twenty-five days' provisions for five persons, some three hundred gallons of water, and five gallons of kerosene.

After putting to sea, they experienced adverse weather and became very sick from eating spoiled food. They had a very hard time of it, but were so intent on saving the lives of their colleagues that they continued their voyage. The skipper, Lieutenant Talbot, died of "excessive overwork" just before reaching Hawaii. On the thirty-first day, the remaining four crew members finally set foot on the soil of Hawaii. Three of the four crew members, however, died soon afterward. Through their noble, sacrificial acts, all their colleagues on the remote Ocean Island were rescued.

As I compared the voyage of the *Natori* boat crew with those of the *Bounty* and the *Saginaw*, I thought about several important differences. They had navigation equipment, well-equipped boats, and a fairly adequate supply of provisions. Further, their voyages were made in peacetime, when there was no fear of encountering enemies by sea or by land. Finally, each voyage involved far fewer men, nineteen in the case of the *Bounty* and five in the case of the *Saginaw*.

In contrast, the *Natori* boat unit had neither navigation equipment nor clocks, a very limited supply of ship's biscuits, the only water for drinking was from rainsqualls, and there was the constant threat of attacks by the enemy. Finally, we began our voyage with 195 men in three boats, which was fifty percent more than the designed capacity of the boats. Lieutenant Kobayashi's thoughtful, decisive leadership and the full cooperation extended to him by the crew were the key factors that enabled the *Natori* boat unit to achieve its goal.

Though fewer days were spent at sea and the distance covered by the *Natori* boat unit was less, I believe that their great accomplishment was as significant as those of the *Bounty* and the *Saginaw*.

Ever since then, I cannot gaze at Orion in the night sky without thinking of the *Natori* boat unit, and meditating on the Western adage "God helps those who help themselves." I appreciate from the bottom of my heart the senior officer present, Lieutenant Kobayashi; without his superb command and leadership, this great event could never have been achieved.

Reflections

Gordon J. Van Wylen

One rewarding by-product of writing this book was to reestablish contact with Captain McMaster. It was delightful to correspond with him. His comments and insights were very helpful as I sought to accurately describe our attack on the *Natori*. I was pleased to learn that in 1950 the navy awarded Captain McMaster the Bronze Star for his part in sinking the *Natori*.

Writing this book brought back memories of my fellow crew members on the *Hardhead*. What a fine group of dedicated, able men to be with in this demanding, dangerous duty. Our executive officer, Capt. Charles D. McCall, USN (Ret), expressed this thought very poignantly in a recent letter to me. "Speaking of submarine crews, we must have gotten the cream of American youth. I surmise that the average age aboard our submarines was about nineteen years. They were really just kids–off the farms and from our cities and colleges. Basically they were untrained and inexperienced, but they learned quickly. Speaking from the experience of four boats and thirteen war patrols, they were great, absolutely tops." These comments also reminded me that fifteen percent of those who served on our submarines during World War II were lost in action.

The USS *Hardhead* was decommissioned on July 26, 1972, transferred to Greece, and recommissioned the H.S. *Papanikolas*, SS114.

The data have been in for a long time and clearly indicate that the ship we sank on August 18, 1944, was the light cruiser *Natori*, and that no other ship was sunk. Theodore Roscoe, reporting this event in his book, *United States Submarine Operations during World War II*, makes this tongue-in-cheek observation: "A submarine on maiden patrol could be forgiven if her eyes dilated at her first engagement and her perspective was a little off."[*]

The unanswered question for us was, What happened to the torpedoes fired during the second attack? Lieutenant Matsunaga has provided some insight through his observation that one of these torpedoes hit the ship but did not explode. Did this happen to all the torpedoes? Did some explode prematurely before reaching the ship? What were the explosions seen and heard from the bridge?

These questions will never be definitively answered. But now that I have become acquainted with Lieutenant Matsunaga, the remarkable journey and safe arrival of the *Natori* boat unit, and the rescue of men from both the rubber raft and the launch, I am deeply grateful that there were no more hits. I celebrate the remarkable accomplishments of the *Natori* boat unit under the superb leadership of Lieutenant Kobayashi and take great satisfaction in the fact that 220 *Natori* crew members survived this event.

As I corresponded with Mr. Matsunaga, rewrote his account of the sinking of the *Natori* and the journey of the boat unit, and relived my participation in these events, a range of thoughts and emotions entered my mind. I frequently found myself fully absorbed in the experiences of Mr. Matsunaga and those with him in the *Natori* boat unit. I felt the hardships they endured, sensed their emotional ups and downs, and shared in their pain as some of their shipmates died. I was in that frame of mind one evening when I spontaneously exclaimed to my wife, "War is really miserable. There must be a better way to resolve issues."

I undertook this writing project because I believed that it was important to have available, in English, an accurate account of the heroic accomplishments of the *Natori* boat unit. But in the process I was confronted anew with issues I had thought about during the war and from time to time since then. How should I think about my involvement in the sinking of the *Natori* and my participation in the war? I now understood, more than ever before, the suffering, hardships, and death that our actions caused. How should I think about war in general, particularly in view of all the conflicts and all the peace efforts since World War II? Faith in God is an important facet of who I am, and Mr. Matsunaga also made frequent reference to a

[*]Theodore Roscoe, *United States Submarine Operations during World War II* (Annapolis, Md.: United States Naval Institute, 1949).

deity. How should I think about faith in regard to these issues?

To help clarify my thinking on these matters, I decided to put my reflections in writing. I remembered that I kept a diary in those days in which I recorded my thoughts as these events transpired. I always intended to read these over, but for reasons I do not fully understand, I never did. Perhaps I wanted to remember only the positive experiences (a human trait that has many positive benefits) and not relive the stresses, hardships, and emotions. Perhaps it was to reinforce the fact that I had closed the book on that chapter of my life, even though from time to time I have related to my family and close friends some of the major events of those years.

This, I thought, was the appropriate time to read this diary. But, alas, though I searched diligently, I could not find it, though I am certain I had carefully packed it each time I moved. I remember its well–brown leather with a clasp and key, which I never used. Perhaps I will find it someday. When I do, I will eagerly read it.

It may be just as well that I did not have it available when writing this book, for it helped me keep the primary focus on the remarkable courage and accomplishment of the *Natori* boat unit and the superb leadership of the senior officer. As for these reflections, they are mine as they have been distilled over the years, now sharpened and shaped as I wrote this book; they are not definitive positions that I present to convince others of their correctness. They reflect who I am as a person–my faith, values, and experiences, as well as the times in which I have lived. These reflections touch three general areas.

The first deals with how I view, almost a half century later, the moral issues that relate to my participation in events such as those described in this book. As I read Mr. Matsunaga's original book and participated in writing this account, I was frequently reminded that those of us on the *Hardhead* were the immediate cause of this tragedy, and that I had had an active part in these events.

I thought again about the context in which this encounter between the *Hardhead* and the *Natori* took place. The attack on the *Natori* was not an isolated event, but was a minor action when viewed in the context of the war between the United States and Japan, which lasted almost four years, covered thousands of miles on land and sea, and cost tens of thousands of lives. My assessment of my involvement could not be isolated from my perspective on the context of the war. And what was this? What had precipitated the war?

The immediate answer was the attack of the Japanese on Pearl

Harbor on December 7, 1941. I clearly remember that Sunday afternoon during my senior year at the University of Michigan when we received this news, and how we were glued to the radio, fully expecting to hear about some decisive victories by our forces. But these victories did not come, and the attack was followed by the defeat of our forces in the Philippines. Congress's declaration of war immediately after Pearl Harbor had my full support, and I was convinced that this action, and pursuing the war vigorously, was our nation's only choice.

The events that preceded Pearl Harbor also had a definitive impact on my thinking. The war in Europe had raged for more than two years before Pearl Harbor. The German forces under Hitler had overrun and occupied almost all of Europe and North Africa, and Japan had conquered Manchuria and much of China. The attitude seemed to be that with adequate military strength a nation could conquer and subjugate other nations at will. The proper role for the United States in addressing these issues was not clear to me, but I certainly felt a moral aversion to these aggressive acts taking place on the world scene.

I also remember the deception and lies involved. One incident stands out in my memory: an afternoon in September 1938, when I sat in our living room with my mother listening to Hitler give his famous Sudetenland speech. His statement, spoken with clarity and the ring of truth, that this was his last territorial demand in Europe made a great impression on me. Afterward I expressed to my mother my conviction that the nations involved should accede to Hitler's request, for this would avoid war and preserve peace. But soon the world knew the reality of Hitler's deception.

Of even greater significance from a moral perspective were the reported atrocities associated with these aggressive expansions of Germany and Japan. Germany's mistreatment of citizens of Norway, the Low Countries, and France stirred within Americans a sense of moral indignation. This mistreatment was better known and is remembered more than some actions by Japan in China and Manchuria before Pearl Harbor, and afterward in the Philippines, Singapore, and Indonesia (then the Dutch East Indies).

All of these were factors in my decision to serve in the United States Navy and volunteer for submarine duty. They provided the context for my conviction that there was a moral basis for the United States to fight this war and for our actions on the *Hardhead* and our aggressive pursuit of the *Natori*. Yes, there were other motives for my volunteering to serve and my pursuit of military success–a desire for adventure, for doing something challenging and even heroic, and a basic competitive spirit to win. But the underlying motive to serve was a genuine belief that there was a moral basis for this war and for my participation.

As I wrote this book I came to the same conclusion as I did at the time of these events: a conviction that ours was a righteous cause, and sadness at the great tragedies caused by war. Yes, war really is miserable. I believe there must be a better way to resolve conflicts between nations and aggressive acts in the community of nations. There is evil "out there" that must be dealt with. The challenge before us, as a world community and each of us individually, is to learn how to do this in ways that are less destructive and more humane.

My second reflection relates to a dimension of war that I see more clearly today than I did when these events took place. There is not only evil "out there" but there is also evil within, which is often more subtle and in some ways harder to handle. One manifestation of this is the tendency during war for combatants to treat it as an athletic contest. The tendency is to keep score–how many ships sunk, how many planes downed, how many tanks destroyed, and even how many enemy killed. The higher the score, the greater the victory and the more medals you receive. During World War II, the navy declared each war patrol conducted by a submarine as "successful" or "unsuccessful" depending on whether an enemy ship had been sunk, and a special insignia was given to those who participated in a successful patrol. I was proud that all six patrols the *Hardhead* conducted were by that standard "successful." But this "score keeping" leads one to think very little, if at all, about the personal dimensions of war, or about the impact of your actions on those human beings called the enemy.

I recall clearly an occasion when the reality of this personal dimension was impressed upon me in a very direct way. In the early 1950s, shortly after I joined the faculty at the University of Michigan, I met a graduate student from Japan who told me about his experience aboard a Japanese ship that was torpedoed by a U.S. submarine. He told me how terrifying this experience had been, and how grateful he was that through the heroic efforts of the crew, the ship got under way and escaped from further attack.

And then I remembered an experience we had on the *Hardhead* on one of our later patrols. We were part of a three–submarine wolf pack that encountered a Japanese ship shortly after daybreak. One submarine in our wolf pack attacked it and achieved a hit on the ship, and as a result it was dead in the water for some time. We were the farthest submarine from the ship, and observed the damaged ship while on the surface some distance away. As the ship got under way, we began tracking it, and after some time Lieutenant Pridonoff and I had determined its course and speed and advised the captain on the right course to intercept the ship. When we arrived at this point, we dove and began a submerged approach. But when the ship changed course radically and passed out of range, I was truly disappointed. Here was a prime target and we had lost this golden opportunity to add to our score. What a tragedy! Had I somehow been negligent in my work and given the captain bad advice?

I do not know whether this was the ship the Japanese student was on. But suddenly this episode took on a new perspective, and our failure to attack the ship was no longer a tragedy, and the score we had been keeping seemed irrelevant. Many lives had been spared, perhaps even that of the friend with whom I was talking.

This perspective has been confirmed as I have come to know Mr. Matsunaga and Mr. Sugahara, and we joined efforts in writing this book. How grateful I am now that the first bow tube salvo of torpedoes we fired missed the target, and that the torpedoes that struck the *Natori* in the second attack failed to explode. I celebrate the fact that between the *Natori* boat unit, the launch, and the rubber raft were more than 220 survivors. Yes, I am deeply grateful that, for reasons beyond our understanding and factors that ran counter to our best efforts, Mr. Matsunaga and I are now friends and coauthors. In war, as in many other facets of life, the score is perhaps significant, but it certainly is not the total story. One must look beyond the score to the human dimensions of war, and realize that those we call the enemy are persons with whom, under different circumstances, we could well be friends.

I began writing this book shortly after Iraq invaded and appropriated Kuwait in August 1990, and the United States and its allies assembled their forces in Saudi Arabia. The first draft of these "Reflections" was written during the conflict, which began in January 1991 with the air war and culminated in the ground offensive that followed in February. Though there was a tendency to "keep score" and count tanks and planes destroyed and the number of prisoners taken, I was impressed that our forces focused on our mission and exercised considerable compassion toward the Iraqi people and prisoners of war.

As I watched on television the treatment given these prisoners, I was reminded of an interesting document I had the opportunity to read. This was the account of the interrogation of the *Natori* survivors on the launch and the rubber raft, who were rescued by the American destroyer and submarine. What struck me was the kindness shown to those survivors and the impact this had on them. Here are two quotations from this interrogation report:

> Ensign ——— (age 20) graduated from Eta Jima Naval Academy in 1944 and immediately went aboard the *Natori* as captain of a 25 mm gun crew. Practically skin and bones when rescued, the unexpected kindness of the crew of the USS *Bunker Hill*, to which he was transferred, the ship's food and the services of the ship's doctor were more than he imagined possible from an enemy. A feeling of gratitude was one obvious reason for his friendly cooperative spirit and his willingness to talk.

> Ensign ——— (Assistant Recognition Officer) was a refined youth of 19, the elder of two sons of Captain ———, Chief of Engineers at Yokosuka Navy Yard. He graduated from Eta Jima Naval Academy in March, 1944. His father was a regular navy officer who instilled in him considerable pride in the service. He was surprised, and somewhat overcome, by the kind treatment received aboard the rescuing submarine, and subsequently throughout his interrogation he experienced a conflict between his desire to remain loyal to Japan and, at the same time, demonstrate his gratitude.

Another reminder of this personal, humane dimension of war came to me recently through a conversation with a person from Austria who spoke with deep, genuine appreciation for the Marshall Plan, the program the United States instituted after World War II to help rebuild Europe. I was struck that this person, born after the Marshall Plan took place, had learned so much about it that he spoke his gratitude with conviction and enthusiasm. My impression is that the policies and practices of the United States toward Japan after the war exhibited much sensitivity to the needs and future of the Japanese people.

Through these experiences and events, and the opportunity to write this book with Mr. Matsunaga and Mr. Sugahara, I was reminded anew of these personal, moral dimensions of war. There is certainly evil out there, and there is also evil within, and it is very easy in war to be overcome with evil. This is why the words of St. Paul still have great relevance: "Do not be overcome by evil, but overcome evil with good." This is an important principle at all times, but particularly during war.

My third reflection relates to the very delightful way in which Mr. Matsunaga included many of his insights and perspectives on life. I am grateful that he included these, for through them we learn much about Japanese life, culture, thought, and values in the 1940s.

As one who has tried to be thoughtful and sensitive in living out his Christian commitment, I was particularly intrigued by Mr. Matsunaga's frequent reference to God. I recognize that Mr. Matsunaga and I come from different religious traditions and that our concepts of God differ. However, it seems to me that we both sensed evidences of Divine Providence.

Why did all the torpedoes we fired on the first bow tube salvo miss the target? Why did the torpedoes that struck the *Natori* on the second attack fail to explode? Why did we observe so many apparent hits in the second salvo when, in fact, there were no hits? How is it that as the *Natori* boat unit was approaching the Philippines, and faced the prospect of being attacked by guerillas, that a Japanese army ship intercepted them and towed them to a friendly base? One can ask similar questions about the submarine that "happened" across the rubber raft and the destroyer that "happened" across the launch.

If we had all the data, we could, at the level of cause and effect, probably answer most of these questions. But would this be the full explanation? I think not, for I see in these events the providence and grace of a God who truly loves us and provides for us in countless ways. Usually the evidences of his grace are found in the ordinary events of life: a healthy body and mind, provision for our physical needs, and loving relationships with our spouse, parents, children, and friends. Sometimes we experience God's love as we receive courage to face difficulties, grace to help those in need, and the ability to receive help when we are in need.

We tend to take these things for granted, attribute our accomplishments to our wisdom and strength, and fail to see in them the love of a God who cares. But dramatic intervention in difficult circumstances can awaken us to the reality that God is concerned and active, and meets our needs in dramatic, unexpected ways as well as in the ordinary events of life.

It seems to me that God's purpose in such events is not only to meet our needs in the moment of crises or extreme difficulty, but also to reveal himself as a God who is there, who cares, and who invites us to experience his presence and grace in every facet of our lives. For me, this perspective comes into special focus in Jesus Christ, who through his life, teachings, death, and resurrection provides the resources for life and death and all that lies beyond.

I appreciated Mr. Matsunaga's final comment on the Western adage, "God helps those who help themselves." From my perspective, I would simply add that God is also the source of our motivation, courage, and strength to help ourselves, and enables us to do so for noble purposes and enduring goals.

Postscript

Following is a brief account of the authors and principals after the events of this book.

HIJMS *Natori*

As ordered by the Navy Department, Lieutenant Kobayashi and the five other lieutenants of the *Natori* boat unit returned to the Japanese homeland from Manila by air. The Naval General Staff was then preparing for a decisive battle at the homeland, and battle-experienced officers were urgently needed. The remaining officers and the crew members were assigned to new duty stations by the Fleet Headquarters in Manila.

Lt. Eiichi Kobayashi

After arriving in Tokyo, Lieutenant Kobayashi reported to the Combined Fleet Headquarters aboard the light cruiser HIJMS *Oyodo*, the flagship of Adm. Soem Toyoda, off Kisarazu in Tokyo Bay. Later he was attached to the Maizuru Naval Base, which was once the home port of the *Natori*.

In May 1945, Lieutenant Kobayashi was promoted to lieutenant commander, transferred to the light aircraft carrier HIJMS *Amagi*, and appointed navigator. His duty aboard the *Amagi* was brief. As the situation in Okinawa was deteriorating, he received his commission as the commanding officer of the Fifth Special Attack Squadron, the 33d Shock Troops, stationed in Aburatsu, southern Kyushu, where 20 *Koryu* (two-man crew midget submarine), 34 *Kaiten* (manned torpedo), and 125 *Shinyo* (explosive laden motorboat) were deployed and ready for surface and underwater special attack against a possible U.S. invasion. Fortunately, the war ended on August 15 of that year, before Lieutenant Commander Kobayashi ordered "Charge!" to his men.

After the war, Mr. Kobayashi worked for two years at the Local Demobilization Liaison Office in Niigata Prefecture, near his hometown. After completing this assignment, he joined the staff of a regional pharmaceutical company.

In 1951, Mr. Kobayashi joined the National Police Reserve, which was organized after the outbreak of the Korean conflict the year before. In 1954, the National Police Reserve was reorganized as the Ground Self Defense Force. He continued in this service until reaching the age limit, and retired with the rank of colonel.

After his retirement, Mr. Kobayashi worked for a pharmaceutical company in Tokyo for twelve years, and at the same time, ran a pharmacy with his younger daughter. He resided in Kodaira City near Tokyo. Mr. Kobayoshi died in 1993 at the age of seventy-five years.

Lt. Ichiro Matsunaga

After returning to the homeland, Lieutenant Matsunaga received orders to report aboard the light aircraft carrier HIJMS *Katsuragi* (a sister ship of the *Amagi*) as communications officer at the Kure Naval Base. In the spring of 1945, the Naval General Staff planned to have the *Katsuragi* consort with the superdreadnought HIJMS *Yamato* and nine escorts en route to Okinawa to carry out a surface special–attack mission without air cover. Her role was to lure enemy aircraft away from the *Yamato* and other ships; this role was later abandoned.

Lieutenant Matsunaga was then transferred to the Naikai (inland sea) Air Flotilla as communications officer, and stationed in the Matsuyama Naval Air Station in Shikoku. He was then stationed at the Iwakuni Naval Air Station, where he witnessed the most unforgettable scene in his life. One the morning of August 6, as he was still drowsing in bed shortly after 0800 (he had stayed up almost all night checking the incoming and outgoing dispatches), he was suddenly awakened by a violent blast. On going outside, he saw a huge explosion mushroom high in the sky to the northeast, toward Hiroshima. It was an indescribable experience, the most dreadful thing he had ever seen. Soon afterward, he learned that this was an atomic bomb. The war ended ten days later.

After the war, Mr. Matsunaga lived in Sasebo City near his hometown, and worked at the Shinwa Bank Co., Ltd. In his spare time, he frequently visited the municipal library and studied the sea and disasters at sea. When he decided to write about the *Natori* boat unit, he found that he had lost his "seamanship" after living on land for almost thirty years and decided he should be aboard a ship for a period to become "salty" again.

Fortunately, he had an interesting opportunity to do so. In 1978, he had an essay published, entitled "Memory of the Navy Blue," which became popular among the Maritime Self Defense

Force. The following year they offered him an opportunity to participate in an around-the-world cruise with the Training Squadron as guest correspondent of their newspaper. They visited thirteen different countries in five months, and Mr. Matsunaga was "salty" again. Inspired by this experience, he completed his book, *The Senior Officer*, the story of the sinking of the *Natori* and the *Natori* boat unit. Published in 1984, this book became a best-seller and there have been twenty printings.

Mr. Matsunaga now lives in Tsurumaki City near Yokohama in Kanagawa prefecture, leading a writer's life.

Paymaster Lt. Dairoku Imai

On leaving the service, Paymaster Lieutenant Imai began a career as an accountant and has served as an executive with an accounting firm in Tokyo. He has also been chairman of the *Natori* Association. Since 1972, ex-*Natori* crew members of various times have held a reunion once a year; a hundred or more former crew members gather each year. Tragically, some of the boat unit crew members died in the Philippine Campaign after their safe return from the sinking of the *Natori*.

Surgeon Lt. (jg) Kiyohiko Togawa

Dr. Togawa, who looked after the *Natori* boat unit crew members at Surigao, has served as a director of the Tokyo Metropolitan Hospital. As he and Mr. Matsunaga had promised, they met each other in Tokyo after the war.

USS *Hardhead*

Gordon J. Van Wylen

While on active duty, Gordon Van Wylen decided to pursue an academic career in engineering. On his release from active duty in February 1946, after completing six war patrols on the *Hardhead*, he immediately enrolled in a master's degree program at the University of Michigan. Because of the influx of veterans into universities, there was a great need for teachers and he had the opportunity to serve as an instructor at Pennsylvania State University while completing his master's degree. This experience confirmed his career decision, and in 1948 he enrolled in a doctoral program at MIT, with a primary emphasis on thermodynamics and cryogenics.

On completing his doctoral degree in 1951, Dr. Van Wylen was appointed Assistant Professor of Mechanical Engineering at the University of Michigan. He taught both undergraduate and graduate courses, engaged in research, and in 1958 published a textbook, *Thermodynamics*, which gained wide acceptance. Subsequent editions of this book were coauthored by a faculty colleague, Richard Sonntag, who had been his graduate student. These books have been translated into various languages, including Hindi, Arabic, and Korean.

Dr. Van Wylen was promoted to associate professor in 1955, to professor in 1957, and in 1958 was named Chair of the Department of Mechanical Engineering. He served in this role until 1965, when he was appointed Dean of the College of Engineering. In 1972, he left the University of Michigan to become president of Hope College in Holland, Michigan, a position he held until his retirement in 1987.

In 1951, Gordon Van Wylen and Margaret DeWitt, a graduate of Duke University and the University of Michigan Medical School, were married. They have five children, all of whom are married, and fifteen grandchildren. Since retiring, Dr. Van Wylen has been involved in various civic and community activities in Holland, where the Van Wylens continue to reside.